In a Fine Frenzy

In a Fine Frenzy

POETS RESPOND TO
Shakespeare

EDITED BY David Starkey & Paul J. Willis

UNIVERSITY OF IOWA PRESS   IOWA CITY

University of Iowa Press, Iowa City 52242

Copyright © 2005 by the University of Iowa Press

All rights reserved

Printed in the United States of America

Design by Richard Hendel

http://www.uiowa.edu/uiowapress

The University of Iowa Press is a member of Green
Press Initiative and is committed to preserving natural
resources.

Printed on acid-free paper

Library of Congress Cataloging-in-Publication Data

In a fine frenzy: poets respond to Shakespeare / edited by
David Starkey and Paul J. Willis.

p.   cm.

Includes bibliographical references and index.

ISBN 0-87745-939-8 (cloth), ISBN 0-87745-940-1 (pbk.)

1. Shakespeare, William, 1564–1616—Poetry.

2. American poetry—21st century.   3. American
poetry—20th century.   I. Starkey, David, 1962–.

II. Willis, Paul J., 1955–.

PR2926.I5 2005

811'.6080351—dc22   2004058869

05 06 07 08 09 C 5 4 3 2 1

05 06 07 08 09 P 5 4 3 2 1

To Sandy and to Sharon

Whose worth's unknown . . .

The poet's eye, in a fine frenzy rolling,

Doth glance from heaven to earth, from earth to heaven;

And as imagination bodies forth

The forms of things unknown, the poet's pen

Turns them to shapes, and gives to aery nothing

A local habitation and a name.

—*A Midsummer Night's Dream* (5.1.12–17)

Contents

In a Fine Frenzy

Introduction

Gathering an anthology of poems devoted to William Shakespeare is a fearsome task — and not just for the editors of such a book. While all poets would like to be compared to Shakespeare, very few ever will be. What sort of writer, we wondered, would be willing to take the height of the one Ben Jonson called "the star of poets"? To what extent, we worried, would current responses to Shakespeare serve mainly to accentuate his greatness, to diminish, by comparison, the efforts of our contributors? And what possible revisionings of Shakespeare could contemporary poets imagine that had not already been attempted countless times?

Somewhat daunted, we looked to see who had gone before us. We found that this genre of anthology has been mainly British, and mainly adulatory. Jonson's "To the memory of my beloved, the Author Mr William Shakespeare" is only the first of many tributes that have been collected and re-collected over the centuries. Jonson has been followed by Milton, Dryden, Keats, Arnold, Swinburne, Hardy, Kipling, Graves, Blunden, and many other notable poets in adding their praises through the years. Typical of the volumes that include these and other, now-forgotten voices is Charles F. Forshaw and Richard Garnett's *At Shakespeare's Shrine: A Poetical Anthology* (1904). The title neatly identifies it within the nineteenth-century tradition of bardolatry, a tradition that persists today. Witness the name of a recent volume by Louis Marder, *William Shakespeare: Nearer My Bard to Thee* (1993).

Bardolatry may be an intriguing subject for literary historians, but poems in this tradition tend to fulsome hero worship — sometimes even when they are written by major poets. To us, a far more interesting project was the *Poems for Shakespeare* chapbook anthology series issued in the 1970s and 1980s by Globe Playhouse Publications and then by Bishopgate Press. Now out of print and rather difficult to find, these chapbooks feature a number of fine British and Anglophone poets, among them Ted Hughes, who begin to register not so much their appreciation of Shakespeare the poet as their interaction with Shakespeare's works themselves. We too wanted to find poets willing and capable of testing, or even challenging, the plays and sonnets. Unfortunately, the only recent collection still available, Anthony Astbury's *Poems for Shakespeare* (1992), reverts to anthologizing historical poems of appreciation. And John Gross's ambitious, eclectic *After Shakespeare* (2002) — dedicated to tracing the influence of Shakespeare upon all manner of writers over the centuries — contains more prose than poetry.

It has seemed good to us, then, to assemble an anthology of poems in response to Shakespeare that are mainly contemporary, that mainly engage the works themselves, and that are mainly American. From this cultural, historical, and geographical remove, we were curious to find out what Shakespeare's poetic stepchildren have made of their inheritance. For, as James Applewhite says of Hamlet in his poem "On the Mississippi," "The river Twain knew / graphs the distance the Dane has to reach / toward us, Old Worlders new // to the silence of landscape...."

Our task set, we found a few of the poems in this volume by contacting likely poets of our acquaintance and combing through various books and journals. But most of the poems came to us through a call for submissions placed in the January 2003 issue of *Poets & Writers* magazine. The avalanche of lively work that descended upon us effectively buried any concerns we might have had that poems in response to Shakespeare could only be derivative.

And there were some surprises. We had imagined a neat volume with poems responding to nearly every play in the canon. What we received were poems that touched upon only half of the full canon. And within that half, our submissions mainly addressed, in addition to the sonnets, just six plays: *Romeo and Juliet, Twelfth Night, The Tempest, King Lear, Othello*, and of course *Hamlet*. Our first reaction was dismay. What was to become of our Platonically perfect anthology, our evenly decorated Shakespearean Christmas tree? Our second reaction was the dawning realization that perhaps the real purpose of our anthology was to take the pulse of this particular cultural moment. In other words, we were finding out what American poets were drawn to, right now, in Shakespeare, and that in itself held fascination.

Granted, the distance Applewhite alludes to hasn't always seemed so vast: the New World has usually been as open to bardolatry as ever the Old World was. From elementary classrooms to graduate school seminars, Shakespeare remains central to our conception of literature. Shakespearean acting companies thrive from Southern California to New England, and nearly every state in the Union has a Shakespeare festival. If most Americans have read only a couple of his plays in high school, many have encountered his work via Hollywood. They've seen Leonardo DiCaprio and Claire Danes as the star-crossed lovers, Mel Gibson or Ethan Hawke as Hamlet. This is not to mention romantic comedies like *Shakespeare in Love* or the numerous "adaptations" of Shakespearean plays for teens — from *West Side Story* to *Ten Things I Hate about You, O*, and *Scotland, PA*. Nevertheless, Elizabethan England and twenty-first-century America are remote indeed from one another in innumerable ways, as the poems we received made clear.

We did wonder, of course, if a number of American poets might be unfamiliar with the canon in its entirety. Possibly so, especially perhaps when it comes to some of the history plays. But we also noted that *A Midsummer Night's Dream* and *Much Ado about Nothing*, two plays that remain quite popular and accessible on stage and screen, attracted very few submissions. What seems more likely than the dark possibility of cultural illiteracy is that some plays leave more to the poet's imagination than others. We received no poems about Beatrice and Benedick, one of Shakespeare's best-loved couples, and very few about Falstaff, arguably Shakespeare's finest creation. Shylock was mostly ignored, as were Rosalind and Kate and Prince Hal. However, we received many poems about Viola, Miranda, Prospero, Desdemona, Iago, Lear, Cordelia, Hamlet, Horatio, and Ophelia.

Especially Ophelia. If we had accepted every Ophelia poem that came our way, they would have drowned this entire book. As it is, we had to turn down a number of very fine ones. Samuel Johnson admits that "Ophelia fills the heart with tenderness." At the same time, however, he famously dismisses her as a "mournful distraction." Similarly, an anonymous critic in *Blackwood's Magazine* in the early nineteenth century complains that Ophelia is not worthy of Hamlet's greatness. Now at the dawn of the twenty-first, it would appear that Hamlet is not worthy of hers. What is it that currently makes her the one Shakespearean character who most firmly occupies our lyric attention?

We have pondered this question and come up with a few rather obvious answers. Perhaps more so than most Shakespearean characters, Ophelia seems to possess a passion and an intellect bottled up and squandered. She is disregarded, marginalized, hemmed in by a host of manipulative men. As such, she has become for us today a potent and tragic feminist symbol. Unlike Cordelia and Desdemona, who are able to defy their fathers, Ophelia is robbed of any sexual or social power. She is left without meaningful connection to others — even to Gertrude — and discovers a sanity only in insanity, finding a voice in madness. Her derangement and suicide are perhaps the felt metaphors for the many ways that women today respond to the pressures of men: eating disorders, self-mutilation, extremes of fashion, feigned imbecility. American poets, we have learned, are mad to give Ophelia a voice at last.

Her importance to contemporary culture is not limited to poetry. In popular music, we note these recent album titles: Toyah Willcox's *Ophelia's Shadow* (1991), The Indigo Girls' *Swamp Ophelia* (1994), and Natalie Merchant's *Ophelia* (1998). Mary Pipher's popular book on adolescent girls in America is fittingly called *Reviving Ophelia* (1994), followed by the spin-offs *Ophelia Speaks* (1999), by Sara Shandler, and *Surviving Ophelia* (2002), by Cheryl Dellasega. We note, too, that a number of our Ophelia submissions are written by men. Men with feminist sympathies, no doubt, but nonetheless men. And we suspect that

Ophelia is not only a feminist symbol but also a symbol of the broadly human predicament of disengagement and disconnection as it is widely experienced in this our time and this our life.

In the body of the anthology, we have arranged the poems in the categories traditionally assigned to the various works of Shakespeare. We begin with poems addressing the sonnets, roughly in their accustomed order. In subsequent chapters, poems about the plays are arranged in the order in which the plays are thought to have been composed. Thus our chapter devoted to the comedies begins with *Love's Labor's Lost* and ends with *Twelfth Night*. Because of the paucity of poems devoted to the histories, we've included the three that fall within this category in the tragedies section. The many poems about *Hamlet* are in their own chapter, and the final grouping consists of poems based on the romances. Individual poems focusing on Shakespeare the man, rather than his work, serve as interludes between each section. Not surprisingly, considering our subject matter, there is a great range of tone from page to page, and a reader unfamiliar with Shakespeare might find the rapid shifts from grief to hilarity disconcerting. Comic poems about tragedies follow decidedly somber poems about comedies, and a single poem may contain a number of emotional twists and turns.

Thus far we may have implied that most of the poems in this volume are character-based. Happily, that is far from the truth. The poets represented here have proven themselves uniquely inventive in their approaches to Shakespeare. Though we have organized this volume, for ease of access, in these rather conventional categories, we could have just as easily grouped the poems by their characteristic strategies and modes of intention.

As mentioned, we do include some poems of homage, as these are inescapable, though we have preferred the sort that sneak up and surprise the reader, such as "Shakespeare as a Waiter," by BJ Ward, or "Shakespeare's Eyebrows," by Sylvia Adams. We have also included a number of tender and humorous poems set in the classroom, where many people locate their earliest memories of Shakespeare. Ron Koertge's "My Students" and Diane Lockward's "On First Reading *Romeo and Juliet*" are good examples of this kind. Many poems, like William Stafford's "Owls at the Shakespeare Festival," locate themselves in the experience of the stage or, like Barry Spacks's "The Film Version," in the experience of the screen. And some poems, like Floyd Skloot's "The Role of a Lifetime," speak from an actor's perspective.

But most of the poems interact directly with the Shakespearean text, and in a surprising number of ways. One response to Shakespeare's high art, and perhaps a particularly American response, is to deflate the text in some fashion. Harryette Mullen's "Dim Lady," a contemporary urban version of Sonnet 130, manages to parody a parody, and J.D. Smith's "Seven Ages of Man" fits Jaques's speech into seven lines. (One somewhat memorable poem that we rejected was titled "Green Eggs and Hamlet.") It is perhaps easy to deflate a text, harder to equal or surpass it. This road less travelled is taken by Michael B. Stillman in his beautiful "Songs for the Seasons: A Distant Collaboration," in which he takes the lovely lyrics on winter and spring from *Love's Labor's Lost* and adds to them his own paired lyrics on summer and autumn. That takes courage.

Many poets are quite overt about finding in Shakespeare a metaphor for their own lives. Cecilia Woloch, for example, sees in *King Lear* an archetype of the challenges of caring for an aging parent. And Katherine Swiggart finds in Mowbray's forced exile in *Richard II* the feeling of a sudden move to a strange place. Other poets, instead of accepting the paradigm of the text, actively resist it, in effect talking back to Shakespeare. Jeanne Murray Walker imagines "How Mother Courage Saves Desdemona," and Reginald Shepherd, in "Snowdrops and Summer Snowflakes, Drooping," orders Ophelia to shut up her singing and get back out of the water. Walker's introduction of Mother Courage offers a related strategy of changing the context. Our poets have great fun with this, as evidenced in titles such as Kevin Griffith's "Hamlet Meets Frankenstein" and Jack Conway's "This Is What Happens When You Let Hamlet Play Quarterback." Yet another form of playful resistance involves what might be called rewriting or extending the text. Thus, in William Greenway's "Ophelia Writes Home" Ophelia reveals how she and Hamlet have escaped to the New World and lived to a ripe old age, and in R. S. Gwynn's "Horatio's Philosophy" the bereaved and bewildered Horatio is rushed along by Osric, Chief of Royal Information, to complete the Fortinbras version of the play.

By far the most traditional mode of response to the text, and still a very fruitful one, is to explore a given character. Sometimes this takes the form, following the lead of Robert Browning in "Caliban upon Setebos," of giving speech to the silent. Kathleen Kirk's "Lavinia" is a most remarkable instance of this, as are many of the Ophelia poems. Sometimes the character is not so much silent in Shakespeare as in some way perplexing to us. Thus, Viola gets her share of poems, and also Iago, and even the perennially hearty Duke Senior in *As You Like It*. And some poems explore their given characters not so much by pushing the boundaries of what might be said by or about them as by dwelling richly in the particulars and circumstances of their supposed existence. These offerings are in the tradition of Tennyson's "Mariana" — a poem, by the way, that Harold Bloom takes great pains to hold up as an example of pure poetry. These languorous, lyrically mysterious poems offer their own kind of delight. Again, many of the Ophelia excursions drift in this direction, as exemplified by Kirsten Dierking's "Delacroix's Version." The connection here to painting is perhaps suggestive of how these poems might best be experienced.

Throughout the selection process, we were aware of the problem Jed Rasula describes in the "Anthologists' Ontologies" section of *American Poetry Wax Museum*: namely, that while most anthologies hope to represent a variety of voices and styles, they nevertheless have trouble conceiving "heterogeneity from outside their own partisan coordinates." Doubtless our own enthusiasms are evident. We favor language that is rich and musical. While we generally shy away from tightly rhymed poems (unless sonnets), we listen for at least the ghost of a meter. And both of us have a weakness for humor — though not always for light verse. Our tastes as editors are similar but not identical. One of us is more open to poems with edge, the other to the traditional. Occasionally one of us would rave about a poem the other heartily disliked. In those cases, the poem was rejected. In general, though, the merits of the poems we chose were immediately obvious to both of us.

There is of course one other thing, besides our editorial taste, that all of these poems hold in common. The very presence of this volume, four hundred years after Shakespeare reached his prime, testifies to the uncanny manner in which he still haunts the ways we encounter our world, even our American world. Whether or not, as Bloom claims, Shakespeare invented the human, we seem to need his constant help to reinvent it as we go. Through the witness of these poets, Shakespeare continues to be just as Ben Jonson would have him: "not of an age, but for all time!" At least, for now — our time.

We wish to thank numerous poet colleagues who have pointed us in the direction of likely poems. Our thanks are also due to the very helpful editors at the University of Iowa Press, to Kate Russell for her inspired secretarial assistance, and to the provost of Westmont College for a generous grant in support of this project.

Prologue

MARVIN BELL

Shakespeare's Wages

Him again, the bard of bards, bard of the boards, he of the company and crew.
He wears a bag of coins, his purse, his recompense, his toll, his confidence.
It's a pigskin bag for one, without a thought of silk, altogether common.
Now he circles the Globe before entering, rebuffing abridgments.
It is his decision to madden Hamlet, his need Ophelia plunging fills.
He has a peasant's legs and a seaman's love of stale bread.
No one but knows of Shakespeare thinks England a dowager Empire.
William himself has achieved respectability beyond London.
That poaching business was the fling of a teen, the record repaired.
A transgression not of bards, but of those whose mouths water for deer.
Oh but William with Histories has conquered all rows and every table.
And Anne, she of the hut down the path, has taken him to her bed.
His characters now suffer in his place, what a life!
There is no questioning it, and his sonnets are something else.

PART I *The Sonnets*

ZACH ROGOW

Symmetron: You and Brother Will

Shakespeare never got to see
a Monet. Never gazed into the liquid mirrors
of the Seine.
Yet he knew how to describe
a sateen shadow.
He could speak beauty
as well as anyone
who has a special ear
for the cool
of a stream or the curves
of a song.

Someone could write a song
about the curves
of your cool,
pomegranate lipstick, how a tongue awakens your ear.
Sometimes it feels to this particular anyone
as if your beauty
is part shadow,
part the highest prime number. I need to describe
you, how you make me crazy and sane
as I look into your eye mirrors
that Shakespeare was never lucky enough to see.

ELLEN MCGRATH SMITH

from Shaken

2

When forty winters shall besiege thy brow,
         a small child will trace the horizontal lines
with alarm and ask inevitable questions.
                       You won't say:
You get credit for half these furrows
         on my forehead. You won't tell the story
behind each crease, or the thwarted ways
         you desired increase.
                   You'll blow out the candles,
leaving some for her, and make a wish to live long enough
         to see another scripture
            make its way across her brow.

3

Look in thy glass and tell the face thou viewest
something that will melt its features down
to what the question is
and always has been.
Can you love me? Or, barring that,
can you love the version of myself
I put on paper?
The question that quickens your heart
when a letter arrives, tears open
the envelope (premature birth
of another rejection). They do not see,
do not see the same face you are trying to make
on this clouded-up glass. Faceless strangers
won't swaddle what, wailing, you bundle
and leave at their doorsteps, won't bend
to the source of the cries, put an end
to this constant deflection.
And so you are furious, sad.
Look at the face and respond to its pleas.
It will never be famous.
It begs your forgiveness.

4

Unthrifty loveliness, why dost thou spend
     all your years pushing pens
across paper? Why not instead feed
     the hungry or even make
money and feather your nest? Why
     do you never stop eyeing the door?
Why is your house in your head?
                              Who put
               your house
     in your head?

LEONARD NATHAN

Making a Love Poem

Let "A" stand for the belovèd, "B"
for a summer's day. Shall we compare them? No,
"A" is more lovely and more temperate —

in short, incomparable, so "B" must do,
"B" a ripe if transient girl — come
with the sun and gone with it in clouds.

Ill-used, she'll wander off, whistling softly
into October, losing leaves, leaving
"A" as yet untouched by human words.

ANTHONY LOMBARDY

Shall I Compare Thee . . . ?

Shall I compare thee to a winter's night?
You are more probing and more fond of fire.
A southern front may dull the blizzard's bite
Or rig with sudden sleet the chapel spire,
The cold may scour our gardens to the ground
Or merely snip their last, bedraggled leaves,
So you, through many turnings, stick around,
Through dawns love greeted and the day it grieves.
While those who fear extinction appeal to fame,
What I still seek in you is something coiled
And secret, more a riddle than a name,
The hours that can't be saved, but can be spoiled,
A pulse, a throw, a quickening of the dark,
Those kisses that hurt but do not leave a mark.

J. D. SMITH

Goodsonnet

after Scorsese

Would you compare me to some kind of clown,
Perhaps amusing to you, good for chuckles,
A goof to lift your spirits when you're down?
Pal, you don't know a blackjack from brass knuckles.

You oughtta see how funny I can be
When some jamoke don't pay up what he owes.
There ain't no punch line like a busted knee —
Ha-ha — or sneezing through a broken nose.

What makes *me* laugh is that some elephant
Agreed to let you borrow his *coglione*
So you could show up here and pull this stunt
In my crew's social club — and you're alone.

It's time for you to learn respect, tough guy.
The lesson goes like this: *Die! Die! Die! DIE!*

LEONARD NATHAN

Ragged Sonnet: When in a Deep Depression

When in a deep depression of the self,
I see on every side, on every hill,
like the lit mansions of the rich, success
of others, hear the echoes loudly praise
my rivals, feel my plodding soles sink deeper
in the cold ashes of hope, and feel
the tepid drizzle of self-pity stain
my cheeks, I think of you, dear friend, who scorned
the Valium prescribed because you thought
sadness was our wise companion, shadow
of later years and not good to deny;
and then, my heart, all but reconciled
to gravity, like a wing evolved for such
short flights, beats up again. But not too high.

LEONARD NATHAN

Ragged Sonnet: So Shall I Live

"So shall I live," the poet said, "supposing
thou art true," but he wasn't referring to you,
who are faithful, but to another woman,
the one whose beauty he likened to Eve's apple
and who, I add here, must have seemed
a cruel emblem of reality,
the way it comes in layers — a frank face
and what's behind that face, another creature
thinking its own thoughts, dreaming dreams
that wake us with a sob. Even you
have sat bolt upright crying your surprise.
There's nothing for it. Apples will be eaten.
"So shall I live, supposing thou art true."
I do not here, of course, refer to you.

JANICE TOWNLEY MOORE

To Love That Well

I have been losing you
all my life.

Until we met
I mourned the void.

Walking with you
in infant spring
I wept the yellow leaves
before the buds matured.

Early, I wove myself
in widow's weeds.

HARRYETTE MULLEN

Dim Lady

My honeybunch's peepers are nothing like neon. Today's special at Red Lobster is redder than her kisser. If Liquid Paper is white, her racks are institutional beige. If her mop were Slinkys, dishwater Slinkys would grow on her noggin. I have seen tablecloths in Shakey's Pizza Parlors, red and white, but no such picnic colors do I see in her mug. And in some minty-fresh mouthwashes there is more sweetness than in the garlic breeze my main squeeze wheezes. I love to hear her rap, yet I'm aware that Muzak has a hipper beat. I don't know any Marilyn Monroes. My ball and chain is plain from head to toe. And yet, by gosh, my scrumptious Twinkie has as much sex appeal for me as any lanky model or platinum movie idol who's hyped beyond belief.

KATHERINE COTTLE

My Poetess' Eyes

for Shelley

My poetess is not blond, like the rest of the world,
or tan from the lamp and credit card.
Her fingers crack and swell from her own bites,
from lists of worries, students, and internal fights.
She is not rich, not quite poor enough to be
a struggling poet, nor the beaten literary whore.
My dear poetess has trouble sleeping
on Sunday nights, smokes when drinking,
and lets the truth blend quietly into lies.
My apologies, Shakespeare, my poetess' eyes
really are two dark ripe almond lips,
her body a young smooth birch, her voice
a cave of aged wheat and the soft noise
of ash through my rough fingertips.

WILLIAM JOHN WATKINS
The Mall

The doors of the mall swing open wide
and streaming in, in search of fashion,
we go like children, screaming, on a ride
at an amusement park. In place of passion
we have purchase, and in place of pride,
credit. This is the church to which we tithe;
the basic hungers can be satisfied
as easy here as holier ground. The scythe
of death put from our mind, a guide
to live our lives by can be found
in catalogues, and stacked on every side
heaven's bounties everywhere abound.
We move as if Time does not have a stop,
but if it does, until it does, we shop.

R. S. GWYNN

Shakespearean Sonnet

With a first line taken from the tv listings

A man is haunted by his father's ghost.
Boy meets girl while feuding families fight.
A Scottish king is murdered by his host.
Two couples get lost on a summer night.
A hunchback murders all who block his way.
A ruler's rivals plot against his life.
A fat man and a prince make rebels pay.
A noble Moor has doubts about his wife.
An English king decides to conquer France.
A duke learns that his best friend is a she.
A forest sets the scene for this romance.
An old man and his daughters disagree.
A Roman leader makes a big mistake.
A sexy queen is bitten by a snake.

RON KOERTGE

My Students

picture Shakespeare just like the domed
bust in Senior English plus puffy pants
and sissy shoes.

They see him sitting in an open window
thinking deep thoughts while below
the Avon teems with life — coal and casks
of wine one way, barges of lowing cattle
the other.

And along the banks, young people kissing
with their mouths open, grappling with
the other's odd clothes,

all the stuff that doesn't make you famous
but that's a lot more fun than poetry.

PART II *The Comedies*

MICHAEL B. STILLMAN

Songs for the Seasons: A Distant Collaboration

Winter (from *Love's Labor's Lost*)

When icicles hang by the wall,
    And Dick the shepherd blows his nail,
And Tom bears logs into the hall,
    And milk comes frozen home in pail,
When blood is nipped, and ways be foul,
Then nightly sings the staring owl,
                        Tu-who . . .
Tu-whit, tu-who: a merry note,
While greasy Joan doth keel the pot.

When all aloud the wind doth blow,
    And coughing drowns the parson's saw,
And birds sit brooding in the snow,
    And Marian's nose looks red and raw,
When roasted crabs hiss in the bowl,
Then nightly sings the staring owl,
                        Tu-who . . .
Tu-whit, tu-who: a merry note,
While greasy Joan doth keel the pot.

Spring (from *Love's Labor's Lost*)

When daisies pied and violets blue
    And lady-smocks all silver-white
And cuckoo-buds of yellow hue
    Do paint the meadows with delight,
The cuckoo then, on every tree,
Mocks married men; for thus sings he,
                        Cuckoo . . .
Cuckoo, cuckoo: O word of fear,
Unpleasing to a married ear!

When shepherds pipe on oaten straws,
And merry larks are ploughmen's clocks,
When turtles tread, and rooks, and daws,
And maidens bleach their summer smocks,
The cuckoo then, on every tree,
Mocks married men; for thus sings he,
Cuckoo . . .
Cuckoo, cuckoo: O word of fear,
Unpleasing to a married ear!

Summer

When strawberries fall by the hedge,
And garden spiders gown the vines,
And melons ripen on the ledge,
And clouds of dust surround the pines,
When spreading crimson ends the day,
Cicadas chide and scrape away,
Skaree . . .
Skaree, skaree: metallic sound
As Marian hoes the dusty ground.

When oven heat makes lovers fools,
And lotus blooms and leafy mint
And roses fresh by mirror pools
Confuse in cooling air their scent,
When aching bones wheel home the hay,
Cicadas chide and scrape away,
Skaree . . .
Skaree, skaree: metallic sound
As Marian hoes the dusty ground.

Autumn

When empty baskets fill the shed,
And rakes' and reapers' season's done,
When leaves are burnt, and Dobbin's dead,
And Marian's nursing her new son;
While Dawn sleeps still, with rosy hair

All tossed and tangled in the briar —

                        A hush . . .

Shhh . . . No infant's cry,
No need another lullaby.

When frost has found the apple bins,
    And empty lies the robin's nest,
When shepherds smile to dream their sins
    And nightmare nags the gardener's rest;
While Dawn sleeps still, with rosy hair
All tossed and tangled in the briar —

                        A hush . . .

Shhh . . . No infant's cry,
No need another lullaby.

DEBORAH LEITER

Midsummer's Eve

The druids and Shakespeare
Had it right, I think —
There's something magic

About walking through the
Reluctantly gathering
Dusk at 10 p.m., something that

Drains the death from your bones

Allowing all the life in you to
Expand outward with the snap
Of a released rubber band, making

You want to simultaneously
Walk twelve miles and kiss
The first stranger you glimpse

LEON STOKESBURY

Bottom's Dream

Methought I was — there is no man can tell what. (4.1.207–8)

I'm the kind of guy who finds himself past midnight
halfway down the frigging kudzu-covered
woodbine-shaded moonlit emblematic forest path
self-conscious to a fault and wondering what
the hell these numerous assorted dead ends
are supposed to tally up to anyway.
                                             "Jesus,
Jesus, Jesus," I have upon occasion in the dark
remarked, but don't think, by your leave,
I ever hung around expecting some response
to such direct address.
                              No.
I may be just the country cousin
forced sometime to city fair
to make a buck and to try my luck,
to tote and grunt, to cart
my baggage, hoist
my wares — my mildewed merchandise,
such as it is and so to speak —
but I ain't that dumb.
                              No
mother's son ever had to explain to me
that we are the zapped, the oblivion riders,
totally lacking — from the first time
that we mewl and cry — even a Chinaman's chance
of knowing the soiled shorts of a sick shyster
from a sack of sugar about the least damned thing.

Observe this bird, that bear, the wild herbs flowing down
yon fecund bank in damp and pearly moonshine.
As they are, so are we: tiny pitiful cogs
which scrape and grind the stars across the sky each night
only for all to dissolve at dawn.

                              And yet,
come morning I am still possessed by these brief
scenes, mists, vapors, frenzied residues.
                              But residues
of what? If man is but a bird, a bush, a bank
where the wild thyme blows; if, as to variations,
'tis all one between the ploughman, who comes and turns
the earth then lies beneath, and this bear
besmirching his face tonight with berries
only to besmear tomorrow his own buttocks with the same;
if all fall down in the great schemata,
why am I left then with these shreds of dreams,
these scraps of hair and hay,
these cobweb patches?
If I could get my hands back down beneath
the muck and stew, back down beneath
these floating fumes —
but such abiding wraiths, such furtive lingerers,
will not disperse. And all attempts become attempts
toward fathoming the unfathomable. Why
how exceedingly erectus, how very
pithecanthropine of me!

Swirling indistinct chimeras, I see them there
drifting up out of their own miasmal goo, from how
far down I think I'll never know, but if I perhaps
could offer to imbue them with the vestments
of this same locale — the vestments, say,
that I might wear me of a summer's day —
might they not then choose
to turn and to expound, having taken on
the accoutrements of said habitat, taking on
its language and its names as well?
And might we then converse us, our same raiments
engendering a commerce that we each could comprehend?
Or would these reveries, like great festering palms
swaying in their orchid fog, despite whatever garb
I might conceive, fold back into the dark quintessence
from which they came, continuing, forever, to exude
only the exotic, the entirely other, the secret idiom
lost in translation, distant, dim, inscrutable still?

EVA HOOKER

What Bottom Said When He Came Home

Please, to wait. It is a week since I have been
in my finished sense. I have had an afflicting sweetness.

Casta diva. Hay in my hair. Ears full of fur.
No one knows who I am.

It's rather like falling off. Sudden, soft.
Up to your neck in chaff and nay-saying.

The dim, odd wood slips through your fingers.
Breathing is dangerous.

Nothing is plain and whole. I remember —
my words are patched.

I do not know the day. It is hard then to know
what to wear. Moss is not suitable. I am in need

of honest neighbors. An apothecary
to hold me even, for I tremble —

like sweet peas in wind.
A tiny mouse walks slowly by my nose,

looks me in the eye, friendly.
I have been made watchful. Is the house secure?

Can I scuttle back? Are there privileges?
I must ratchet down the windows. Milk the cow.

If we light the lamps, we will see each other's faces.
You bend over the fire.

Your elbow is startling, delicate as bread
and flowers. Your hands are warm.

Grief does not cling to my skin.

I have two lives now: then, and then.

I know now — plain song is fragile, a privacy
trained to fold like an envelope. Your hair smells of dust.

I must lie down. When my cue comes, call.

KATHLEEN KIRK

Portia

They came from far and wide
to match me
in the dad-rigged game,
that old romance.

I liked the one
with looks and brains,
nothing new.
He liked me, too.

I said the old words,
sang the old songs,
then, to save a life,
I brought down the house.

Newspapers verify such things:
a mother saves her child
by lifting up a car.
Not me: my brain stalled,

lips jammed,
and into black nothing
came something like rain
and fire mixed.

Yes, I was a volcano!
Blood of earth slid down
my body, devastating nothing,
not one pound of flesh.

How did I do it?
I was the great poem we hope
will not improve
with subsequent revisions.

I was inspired by love,
yes, the old game,
the old words, the gentle
rain that washes us clean.

J. B. MULLIGAN

Shylock

Looking up into Leviathan,
the deep and gaping dome above the nave
with fangs of beams and shadows threatening
to fall upon him in a frenzy of
devouring faith, the Jew, his ancient back
bent upon the unforgiving lip
of the cold baptismal font, his red, shaved cheeks
fluttering like gills, groaned and flapped,
unable to escape the merciful hands
of laughing, praying Christians, as the priest
and lost Jehovah both ignored him, blind
and deaf to every curse and plea. He gasped
as water burned the furrows of his face
and marked him party to his own disgrace.

PETER MEINKE

Blow, Blow, Thou Winter Wind

Then heigh-ho, the holly!
This life is most jolly. (2.7.182–83)

In my criminal stage I fell in love with Bert
who did an awkward handstand in her skirt
that sent the Sage girls gasping from the room
This was the fifties: life could be shocking then
and I lived like a pig in the college dorm
reserved for Jews and other exiles   Bert moved in

on weekends   A Polish boozer in
love and hate with God she'd mime His voice: *Bert*
hast thou dropped thine pants again? Thou die! The dorm
hall echoed as she trilled slipping her skirt
and shoes and jumping on the bed then
calling for wine or vodka as if my room

were some East Village den   In truth the room
was smoky sticky vile sweatshirts festered in
dank mounds ashtrays stank   She'd flip the stolen thin-
stemmed glass over her shoulder: Bert
liked to think we had a fireplace   Later we'd skirt
the shards of glass in our bare feet blow the dorm

and saunter through the snow while half the dorm
hung out their windows cheering   There wasn't room
for coyness in our act: she'd flap her wet skirt
back at them take my arm and heads high in
we'd go crashing some Christmas party where Bert
would lean on the piano while I cadged drinks   Then

pure as any Shakespeherian maid sing *Then*
heigh-ho, the holly! under a lion dorm-
ant on a shield: *Semper liber* Ah Bert
you were beautiful in those heraldic rooms

your long-lashed umber eyes drowning in
music And I would clown sprawled before your skirt

your bare toes tapping out beneath that skirt
their fragile SOS a neurasthen-
ic code I hopelessly misread seeing in-
stead only your fine frenzy If later in the dorm
you curled weeping in my arms the room
tight with shadows I should have whispered *Bert*

although this squalid dormitory room
squats in the skirts of hell your presence here
is holy Bert God loves us now and then

J. D. SMITH

Seven Ages of Man

I puked and cried — that's what Mom said.
School sucks. Why can't I stay in bed?
I want that girl. What is her name?
I'll kick some ass and stake my claim.
I'm fat. So what? I've won the game.
I limp these days, and feel the gout.
Say, now, what was all that about?

LEON STOKESBURY

Jaques Lured by Audrey

As the ox hath his bow . . . (3.3.79)

I swear I know not how, but as fleeting as
ice sculptures melting on a summer lawn,
opalescent in moonlight, winking like dark jade
out on the damp grass and away, these globes
of memory dissolve right down into the earth
as quick as all these goat droppings will in rain.
This very forest floor must be engorged by now
with generations of droppings, but no one sees
or cares. And how it happened I do not know, but
since that brief merger, since we pleasures proved,
O my adult arcade, my nut-brown study, my sylvan
nocturne in burnished beige and gold, it has been
like knocking on the deaf man's door of my brain
to thrust anything through there but that one moment,
this stopped dot of you growing more obscure each day,
your goat-reek rank on my hands like fresh garlic
and mint from the garden. How banish this dot
of you! Even though the thought itself is black
ink turning brown, this want will not burn down.
It flares in here, a never-flickering auto-da-fé,
an urge that will not purge, forever a hunger
nearly gnawing its way out. Banished now from
my own being, swaddled all in motley now, my
only wear — might we, together, be that beast
again, crushed mint, garlic, reek, balm, that ram,
O my tiny *Temptation of Saint Anthony*, together
might we make once more our common, curful cry.

GILBERT ALLEN

The Good Duke Speaks

And this our life . . .
Finds tongues in trees, books in the running brooks,
Sermons in stones, and good in every thing. (2.1.15–17)

The epilogue was hers
because she didn't want me to spoil it
and I didn't want to disappoint her.
It was a small enough thing.

Lord knows, she'd had things
hard enough for her already:
wandering the woods, dressing up
like the boy I'd always wanted

her to have been. But now I want
to say something, since everyone's
putting stones in poems these days,
although they'd never build my church

with them. What's a church
got to do with all this?
Well, nobody knows the good
in everything, but you have to say it

and if you say it
enough, it may
turn into a forest of phrases
you can worship, true

or at least a bit truer
than before you lied.
What was my daughter's virtue
but deception?

She learned this deception
from me, though I never let
her know it. I'm not as stupid
as you think,

my brothers, though you think
it each time you return
to my words. My adversity
was sweet, I tell you,
and I used it well.

DANIEL WILLIAMS
Feste and the Fence Post

Madman, thou errest. I say there is no darkness but ignorance. . . . (4.2.42–43)

This old fence will speak its piece
In voice of rusted moss   it speaks
Of wormwood crisply light
Broken gates   old firebright spots
Now black as coalsilk night

Listen and you will hear ballads
Of the wind in knots and splits and
Swollen grain   warm textures of a
Soul that dreams this glow of old wood
And if I could I'd learn its turning

Now Stellar's jay grasps one noisy post
M'lord in blue of dart and shout
He sees two fools who spend
Their lives in wooden strife
Who hold things in or keep them out

SANDY FEINSTEIN

The Catch

Snatches of the Fool's songs
catch in my throat:
"Come away, come away"
I sing to myself.

"In sad cypress let me be laid"
I self-dramatize with tears.
I wonder if I sang aloud
could I beg as well as he?

Sometimes even Feste looks sad.
Some say, it's the threat of loss,
others, that he's been crossed.
I say, it's what can't be said
by a fool left alone on stage.

MARY MAKOFSKE

Viola, to Olivia

Olivia: *I would you were as I would have you be.*
Viola: *Would it be better, madam, than I am?* (3.1.142–43)

In Cesario's breeches, I fell in love
with swaggering. Under a cocked hat
my wit came loose, my words made flesh
tremble. I walked dark streets and learned
to laugh aloud. Though you slipped,
supple as a lie, into my brother's bed,
you won't forget the way I wooed.
Sister, it was not in spite of
my soft cheek you loved me.

CHRIS TERRIO

Viola Recalls

New, the feel of sand after sea
has made its case, has made itself
the first thing, then how all things
are held interlocutors, difficult,
their argument solidity. Listen:

it is always a beginning. It is always
a between — thing, recognition, thing.
This is becoming. This is where
(do not mistake this for philosophy)
things begin. To come back, then,

is difficult. Resurrection has more to do
with protest than beauty, even flowers, even
trees, here and here and here, against earth,
its heaviness, its final decision.

There is a knowledge that precedes.
A showing, a foregone conclusion.
That long before the shore I had arrived.

MELANIE KENNY

Hungry as the Sea

Dead leaves scent the hall with nutmeg.
The soldiers are in the bunkhouse.
The courtiers have gone home, drowsy
with gossip from the day's unveiling.
No one sees the slight boy-shape in the corridor:
feet bare, boots in hand, sword left on her bed.
She moves slow, undoing
the past few weeks of walking like a man.
His door carved with grinning foxes opens.
In the sudden bright, he seems lost to her
until his breath heats her neck:
My Cesario, my delicious boy —

Bodies in navy-issue broadcloth,
plain white shirt fronts, breeches both.
Before he knew her truths, the same
thin black leather belts clasped their waists.
She could not have him, she had thought,
only glean a bit by living in his clothes —
the world on her skin just as it must be against his.
Fingers on brass buttons fumble for the known difference.
He unbinds her chest, spins her from male to female.
His mouth is softer than hers, softer than any woman's.
In the tremendous burst of feasting,
the wreck returns to her.
She feels the ocean pulling within her belly.
I have swallowed the sea, Orsino.
She bites his shoulder. He sucks her salt.
Mine is all.

BJ WARD

Shakespeare as a Waiter

He was tired of the old ladies
        wanting cappuccino, of the little kids
with their chocolate milk or *two* cherries
        on a plastic dagger — anything to consume
his time while he had more important things
        to do — a fair lady in booth three was dying
for a reuben, and twelve lit professors
        wanted another round of ale and song in the lounge,
and his entire tip probably depended on it.
        This is where he started to learn timing —
when to allow the waiting, when to deliver
        what will last a while.
His boss started yelling — "Shakespeare!
        Bus your tables!" He was tired of this too.
He was tired of picking up and wiping down,
        tired of people's half-eaten burgers,
tired of salad dressing, tired of the spit,
        tired of the cooks who called him "Willy"
all day, tired of directing people
        to the bathroom when he had so much more
direction to offer. But he didn't reject this —
        none of it. Instead, he took it in,
studied it until he understood it.

In his mind, things grew large —
        first nothing, then nothing
became an ocean
        dotted with islands —
each island had a name —

        Venice, love, Denmark —

                a dark count started to form,
        witches sang,
                stars crossed,

and Shakespeare,
       between the napkins and ketchup,
   lit a table's candle
and waited for the evening shift.

PART III *The Tragedies (and Histories)*

KATHLEEN KIRK
Lavinia

I'll be a small brown bird
that doesn't sing.
You will know me
by my ragged wing.

Catch me if you dare
assault the air!
Catch me if you can,
woman or man!

I'll be a kite
broken on the tree.
I'll be a star
sliding to the sea.

When you see me,
wish for good.
Then do it.

You are the second,
I was the first
chance.

There is the music,
take my lack
and dance.

MICHAEL B. STILLMAN

The Two Princes

Men

who cannot eat dried oats, who
cannot draw carts
will find men's work, so
Richard procures

Tyrrel, who
procures
Dighton and Forrest, who
procure

— their shadows curved behind them, sharpened
on the stones as they descend —

indifferent, impersonal
the keys,
the means to murder.

Quietly, they rise
to enter
the bedchamber, these
hallucinations of procurement.

What minds can keep their luster
comprehending
the continuous assuagement of horror which fashions to perfection
such instruments

of irresistible
power
— so remote and so pure?

Innocence
in the softness of those children
lay

dreaming.

KATHERINE SWIGGART

The Exhaled

What is thy sentence then but speechless death,
Which robs my tongue from breathing native breath? (1.3.172–73)

She answered the phone and heard her answer.
　　No heavy breathing, no Firemen's Relief,
　　　　no final reprieve — only the sentence:
　　　　　　You will be exiled from the sounds you know.

Something like this had happened before
　　when she was talking to herself somewhere
　　　　in a park, or a tree, or on a stage
　　　　　　playing the castaway, hundreds of years

before speech became Required Reading.
　　Here then is her unstringed testimony:
　　　　At midnight they brought me to the station.
　　　　　　A man gave me a ticket to Not Here.

I was driven away from the city
　　in a long orange car with a high roof.
　　　　If there was treachery, I won't say whose,
　　　　　　but something like this had happened before

en route to Charles Brown Junior High School
　　when words were flung, harsh, inarticulate —
　　　　early notes of American Music.
　　　　　　The high car moved slowly from town to town

stopping until no seats were empty.
　　I sat between a window — or widow —
　　　　and something four-legged, a chair or dog.
　　　　　　Passengers were each permitted one bag,

or "sack" as they say where I'm living now.
    Mine held a wooden model, made to scale,
        of the House of Speech it had taken me
            forty years to build. I'm in the east wing.

The rooms are small here
    and oddly appointed,
        and sawdust shows where
            walls have been shortened.

DIANE LOCKWARD

On First Reading *Romeo and Juliet*

While the rest of us read the death scene,
you twirled your gold-red hair, red
like the inside of a pomegranate,
spun it around
your index finger
in spirals.

        Maggie,
you didn't know that in a certain light
sun motes glinted
off your hair, not quite copper,
not quite bronze, but something
more rare.

When the bell rang right in the middle
of Romeo's final soliloquy,
you closed your book and tossed
your tresses, all fourteen-year-old
nonchalance, then strolled past Jimmy Dimouli,
the dumb kid who'd read the part of Romeo
you'd ignored.

You made your exit like a star, hair
trailing behind — a fiery comet
showering particles of gold
at Jimmy's feet.

        Maggie,
you didn't notice him, star-struck,
spiraling like a solar wind toward Earth,
half a soliloquy stuck in his throat.

TANIA RUNYAN

Teaching Shakespeare

They hold no loyalties to the star-crossed lovers,
their books resting lightly in their hands, pencils tapping,
urging me to gallop apace so the two can put themselves
out of their misery.
               It's nothing but a lust story;
he saw her work those curves in some circle dance,
and that was it.
              I press: is it possible? Is it remotely
conceivable that they loved?
                  Hey, we go to parties
and check each other out. We know nothing
about love. But we'd never die for looks
like those morons.
              They all nod in agreement, and I fear
the slow, dreadful flowering of the remaining scenes,
the doodling, the glaring out of windows, my own
growing conviction that Romeo would have played the field
if he had lived three more days.
                  The class genius stares desperately
at his neighbor's blonde ponytail, then blurts,
So who's this Tie-balt?
            to her melodious laughter.
I can only look down and smile, remembering my own foolish fortune,
when I allowed my mind to sculpt itself
around a startling green eye, or a lock of hair hanging over
a boy's forehead.
             I wish I could tell them, it's all true —
all of it. We know nothing about love for a long, long time.
I wish I could tell them how I rode my bike a mile
out of the way to catch a glimpse of Teddy at his basketball
hoop; how I hid my perfect trig scores from Kevin;
how for David, I ringed my eyes with so much smoky shadow,
they watered;
            how for no love at all I took a little of my life
every day.

BARRY SPACKS

The Film Version

It must have been Tom Stoppard,
that Shakespearean wag,
who thought to have a stuttering actor
play the Chorus, in what once was called
Romeo, and Ethel the Pirate's Daughter.

"Two households, both alike in dignity" —
the first pentameter just won't emerge! —
the actor burbles, ticks, he glots,
but then, O wonder, now he's off . . .
each time I watch this scene I weep

over blockage turned to eloquence;
Old Bill himself would have loved the trick,
like to the lark at break of day arising
and Juliet granted years beyond all woe
with this her deathless Romeo.

SHEROD SANTOS

Romeo & Juliet

O true apothecary! (5.3.119)

With that same unsettling instinct for how
Human love can fall by chance to the borrowed
Grave of a coldwater flat, the forecast snows
Heaped up since dawn against our two small

Street-level windows, walling out the staticky,
Offstage noise of the early morning traffic,
The stink of trash and exhaust pipe fumes.
But when setting aside our breakfast trays,

And drawing the goose-down coverlet off,
You climbed up over me, late for work,
And filled my mouth with a nut-brown,

Poppied aureole, I couldn't believe that either
Of us would ever die, or that, given the choice,
We wouldn't choose this and be buried alive.

DANUSHA LAMÉRIS DE GARZA
Act One

They are ordinary, here. The man, lying in the metal bed
a mask over his face, eyes looking up, unfocused, his head smooth, freckled
the woman looking down at him, her hand in his, keeping pace

with the stranger in loose green clothing who pushes the bed through the
open doors
of the elevator. There are spectators, a group of them, listless
waiting for the doors to slick open, then close, for the hospital to swallow
them inside.

It is a common scene, Romeo and Juliet, the balcony.
She, calling out to him, his answer, the east
the bright sun, her face, and now this woman, playing her

silently calling out to the man in the metal bed, "Romeo, Romeo," etc.
as if she could summon him from the depths of the morphine, that elegant
darkness, and into the bright light of the elevator, as if he would

call back to her, as if, when the doors opened on the second floor
to the crisp sound of applause, they could walk away from all of this forever.

H. PALMER HALL
Romeo Is Dead

for Bob C.

I was Capulet, he Romeo,
my daughter the target of his lust.
Just fourteen, she simpered, pouted.
Her nurse, hands full, delighted
in her wish to rid herself of that
slight tissue that would make her
marriageable to a Parisian count.

Years later I read about him,
this Romeo, young handsome man
that I remembered from school,
romantic, love writ large upon his face.
His Juliet still lived, settled into
matronly mediocrity, two sons
in law school, a daughter married to
a teacher at the local college. Juliet
pickets abortion clinics in her spare
time, sells cosmetics for Mary Kay,
hosts each year a Tupperware party
for a highly select few dozen friends.

But Romeo had a brighter life,
strutted his hour upon the stage.
I read about him in the local paper:
"Actor, 42 years old, best known
for playing a crack addict on *Hill
Street Blues*, of AIDS. New York,
September 13, 1992." Romeo
is dead and Juliet doesn't care. She
reads the paper, thinks of him
beneath her balcony, smiles, dreams
they married, made love when she
was just fourteen, a kind of rape,
and died together in her family tomb.

When the quilt came to our town,
I searched closely for his name and
found it, obscure, one among many,
not at all like the man who saw Juliet
in the east and thought he saw the sun.

JACKSON WHEELER

Falstaff's Dream

Was I asleep? I think more about sleep
now than I did when my arm was agile
and there were drinks enough for all.

I dreamt I stood waist deep
in fragrant barley near the ruins of Tintagel
alert to young Hal's plaintive bugle call.

Who knows the why of dreams
or why I ventured so far west
except for genuine love of the boy.

He never truly understood, it seems,
how passion makes a man attempt his best
yet rue the day he longed for a soldier's joy.

BJ WARD

Daily Grind

A man awakes every morning
and instead of reading the newspaper
reads Act V of *Othello*.
He sips his coffee and is content
that this is the news he needs
as his wife looks on helplessly.
The first week she thought it a phase,
his reading this and glaring at her throughout,
the first month an obsession,
the first year a quirkiness in his character,
and now it's just normal behavior,
this mood setting in over the sliced bananas,
so she tries to make herself beautiful
to appease his drastic taste.
And every morning, as he shaves
the stubble from his face, he questions everything —
his employees, his best friend's loyalty,
the women in his wife's canasta club,
and most especially the wife herself
as she puts on lipstick in the mirror next to him
just before he leaves. This is how he begins
each day of his life — as he tightens the tie
around his neck, he remembers the ending,
goes over it word by word in his head,
the complex drama of his every morning
always unfolded on the kitchen table,
a secret Iago come to light with every sunrise
breaking through his window, the syllables
of betrayal and suicide always echoing
as he waits for his car pool, just under his lips
even as he pecks his wife good-bye.

JENNIFER HILL KAUCHER

Reading *Othello* and Watching a Girl Skip Rope

Mouthing a rhyme about ivy
or a handkerchief fallen,
the rope swings and arms circle
like time in otherworldly whips.

The girl plays alone on asphalt,
under the unforgivable blue sky,
for better or bitter left to her devices,
tapping the sureness of the world with rope,
body leaping, airborne for an instant,

her grip tightens on the handle,
braids released like wings —
the boys led by their longing
to this girl, a strumpet, trumpet
out loud in the open yard.

What girl will count her sins
aloud when she can only go
as far as seven? The cord warps
midair on love, love.
Not high enough for joy,
low enough for God.

CHAD DAVIDSON

I Took by the Throat the Circumcised Dog

This is why we read: this same tragedy
of Shakespeare just beyond
my body's yard-length grasp.

When I recall my father
raise his voice to prop *Othello*
on his breath, I curl around, meaning

I'll stay to hear the final blow,
which punctuates this drug called
play. We're trained. Still these

tricks, these variations spun
in circles like the dogs we are before
we lay them down on paper. Words rattle

in their rooms, doubloons held back
for fear we couldn't stand all that
emptiness: this is why we read.

This dog I drive along does not believe
the delphic yelp of birth-
right neat in stainless scalpels,

the ins and outs of suture.
I scan graffiti in pentameter
while instinct — which is always wrong

and perfect — tells me not to.
But we are smitten thus: forgive me,
Father, you who never read me

Shakespeare, never knew *Othello*.
Like myself, it's sitting on its stand.
I have never read it. I do not think I will.

CARMEN GERMAIN

Literature 100

Iago had his reasons,
but still we wonder
why he did it —
the fisheries students
who'd rather watch the video,
the engineering major
who calls Desdemona
that sleaze ball,
the nursing student
who keeps saying
It's all easy, it's all just
soap opera —
why he stunned the Moor
with innuendo's rag of grief,
handkerchief with its pure seam
of blood, each thread embroidering
a new womanly sin,
each whisper, each glance
pointing its finger
anywhere but straight,
the cracked-cup universe
finally put on the table.

ARTHUR POWERS

Iago

Hazlitt calls Iago an artist. And
So he is. The pains he takes to create
Destruction — intricate patterns of hate
Wrought for love of hate by a master hand.
Perhaps it is a bit unfinished, poor
About the end, imperfect, impure — one
Wife's loose tongue, one undoing touch undone.
Yet who will deny the ruin of the Moor?
The beauty of its subtlety, the play
With men's lives: tragic plan of demanding
Evil. Surely some Venetian standing
About the twofold funeral must say:
"This was the master's last great work before
He swore himself to silence evermore."

J. P. DANCING BEAR

Iago, the Poet

First, let me say it is sickening, this syrupy public
adoration for being homespun and common
tongued, master of the art. I tire of his shotgunning metaphors
to stuff and mount on his study wall.
Last night I convinced a group of drunken bards to burn a pile
of his essays and his effigy while slamming down more beer
and shouting, *You're not our leader!* Today I made the surrealists
believe he would come after them next and they should join
the language poets and attack first. I've tricked his confidants
into thinking he's used them. I have convinced his fans
he's insincere, a stage-clambering phony who borrows
ideas, has roots in the greeting card business. But my best
yet was swaying him to see his great love as a cheap
whore for hacks, charlatans and poseurs; and ruin his own career.

R. S. GWYNN

Iago to His Torturers

The time, the place, the torture, O, enforce it! (5.2.369)

Tighter, me boys! One half-twist on that screw
And the wee piggy'll pop like a green bean.
Tighter, I said. And if the bloody shoe
Won't fit, ah, make it fit. My foot, I mean.
Let me my tendons plink, boys, lovely boys.
Tune up the rack. I love it, every minute.
Enjoy me whilst you can, like kids with toys.
Remember, I won't have to face the Senate.

And when the Maiden's fired, while hoists and cranks
Pinwheel me like a flea-bit dog-day dog,
Maybe you'll get it, how I did it so
We'd come to this, who like my pleasure slow.
Say Emilia wasn't handy with the flog.
It's all in the wrist. For this relief, much thanks.

JULIAN BERNICK
Iago

Just once,
As I looked
At that silver knife of a lake,
Sheathed in trees,
While my fingers combed
The greedy breeze for nothing,
I felt something rise
From the cold holster of my soul:
It occurred to me

I might mean something.

RACHEL BECK

Interlude

Sing together.
Who shall lead, who
follow?
In the green brush,
in the hollow,
willow.
On this evening
face wept pale-clean
lady's
tears salt her voice
near to broken
choking
on stiff stems of
green green garland
willow.
Branches breaking
in a hot wind,
Cyprus
and Othello.
Who shall lead, who
follow?
Emilia hears,
murmurs mellow,
offers
small hand comforts
sweet to swallow:
lady
you are not well —
rest, head on my
pillow.
Emilia, too,
sings, thin-candled
chill. Oh,
her own song spins
to tear-streaked gold
willow.

RACHEL BECK

Epilogue for Emilia

Perchance, Iago, I will ne'er go home. My bones
by their drained-limp pile, should say: home never was. A name
at most, a few damp curtains in autumn. This floor, this pool
of blood where cells of wavering shimmer break to drops —
but I digress. Go cut your tongue with sharp-tooled will.
You've webbed yourself, and in those threads I see you lie.
But I have vowed a revocation, stricken from light
as the new moon. I cannot weep for home; my dimming eyes
see in her hair a softer shroud than all old promises.
The seabirds outside wheel and call as if pierced by wind.
Give me a shawl. My knotwork now undone, I,
in my green candle's haze, shall stitch a winding border:
the fine lace squared and scarred with love-lies-bleeding.
I leave my kerchief and my hand, both worth the needing.

DAN JOHNSON

Maybe Desdemona

If what she heard is true
the dead are only sleeping.
Tomorrow night in another town
the tent unrolls in a field,
drifts and settles and steadies.
Men who surround her with greasepaint
have something to give for pain,
a simple black slash extending an eyelid,
flecks of gray in the hair
she unpins, uncoils backstage.

Maybe Desdemona only sleeps
in a place defined by torches,
when a crowd comes to fill
the shipwrecked wooden bleachers.
Then she can rise and walk away
behind the settling curtains,
leaving us to search for shelter
with the others, and for sanctuary
from the wind that scours a field
or ebbs to shallow breathing.

JEANNE MURRAY WALKER

How Mother Courage Saves Desdemona

for Susan Sweeney

Desdemona is sobbing in the bedroom, a hole
in her heart, when Mother Courage strides in
wearing black-tie shoes, to switch on the lamp.

She has just driven her wagon across Europe
to find her dead daughter, Katrin,
stripped the body to sell her shirt, and then

walked aimlessly all night. At the door
of a theatre she hears a young woman sobbing.
Tenderly she whispers, *Here, Little Sausage, blow*

on your hem. She wants to pull Desdemona from
her extravagant belief in her own downfall.
Because what is a handkerchief, the old woman asks,

but a certain way of thinking about the world,
a flutter in the wind, anybody's wind.
If you aren't careful, you nest in one man's pocket

and then whoosh, you turn up in another's.
But you are a precious clue, the only real thing
in the play! You can't trust a man

whose name begins with O! When he mutters,
Turn out the light, Sheepface, Daughter, Desdemona,
YOU are the light! Given what that Moor did,

you should be ashamed to leave a trail of boohoos
like snail tracks across Europe!
Get up! It's time to find another play.

Mother Courage goes on scrubbing past romance,
down to the very floorboards of love.
Together they rise. Now they are walking past us

down the aisle, exiting the theatre
to find their own lives, sheltering hope
in their hands as if it were a cup of tea.

WILLIAM STAFFORD

Owls at the Shakespeare Festival

How do owls find each other
in the world? They fly the forest
calling, "Darling, Darling."

Each time the sun goes out a world
comes true again, for owls:
trees flame their best color — dark.

At Shakespeare once, in Ashland,
when Lear cried out, two owls
flared past the floodlights:

On my desk I keep a feather
for those far places thought
fluttered when I began to know.

STEPHEN COREY

Understanding *King Lear*

When you stir
the blueberry yogurt —

spoon down through
the white cultured yogurt
to the syrup and fruit
underneath,

dark bluepurple rising
first in bursts of color,
then swirling as you stir
into designs of thin-lined
purple and white,

distinction fading
to a deep magenta cream
lumped with blue,
magenta-covered berries —

imagine
Shakespeare's life,
the daily incidents,
the human brilliance.

ANN LAUINGER

Three Songs for *King Leir*

Note: In Shakespeare's sources, the old king and his daughter survive.

1. Cordeilla

Where nothing grew I set a knot of herbs,
Wholesome plants — hyssop, thyme, rue.
Afternoons, he dozes in the sweet air.

Against the stone walls I espaliered roses.
I have watched the bees, flashing gold
While he sleeps, halo his white hair.

Green throat of summer, you are only a flourish
Of my sole monarch, my familiar root.
Nothing begets in me; I am nothing's heir,

Impatient to come into my kingdom. When the bees,
Blurring like smoke, sail off to hive themselves
In oak, when soil and stone are laid bare

I seat him by the fire, steady the cup
As he drinks, rub his feet. Then there are
His hair and beard to trim, his nails to pare.

2. Leir

Unstring the harp
Beat the hedges
Rid me of the lark
Thrush linnet
They will not
Peace at my bidding
Their music kills me
Let fall

When I would sleep
The nightingale sings
No cause, no cause
Find out who taught her
Whip him straight
She should be Gorgon-voiced
So I a man of stone
Her music kills me
Let fall

He that catches me
A pair of crickets
To scrape their legs
When I am merry
Or a leathern bat
Shall squeak me lullabye
I will thank him
For my music
. Let fall

3. Edgar

Who can I tell? I miss my disguises.
Simply myself, I shall never be as wise as
Poor Tom or as strong as the Black Knight
Avenging Father's eyes, thwarting his suicide.
My clumsy self, briefly without a part,
Blurted out truth and stopped the old man's heart.

I hereby vow, for all the old men's sake,
To banish truth. Life is a dream; we wake
Only to execution. The old king
Shall not so much as stub a toe. Nothing
Arresting, unyielding, not the mildest friction
Shall touch him. Grant me, gods, the gift of fiction.

JOAN RAYMUND
The Ordeal of Love

> *I love your Majesty*
> *According to my bond, no more nor less. . . .*
> *Sure I shall never marry like my sisters,*
> *To love my father all.* (1.1.92–93, 103–4)

Cordelia, we needed more from you.
Why couldn't you give old Lear
the luscious words he longed for?
Say you'd but suffer a husband in your bed,
pretend a fondness for any get you got?

Why all this rot about lying?

Too busy all his kingly years for family stuff
what with business deals and conference calls
and rough armies to assemble,
Lear could not hear the voices of children
with a cellular slapped to his ear.

Now he asked but the trappings of love,
gold-seeming coins for his coffer.
Why couldn't you make the offer?

O Child, lying is the miracle
that holds our leaky lives together.
Am I still pretty? whispers dismantled wife.
Was I so stupid! man shoots darkly
from the sagging porch.
We pour the words that fill them.
Anything less would kill them.

You should have done as much for Lear,
who might have died in old man's bed.
And you — not hung from a cruel thread —
prim mouth agape for any kiss.

BRIAN STAVELEY

Speak Again

Trapped like Cordelia's heart, tongue-tied inside
Her chest, the mind finds no egress. Belief
In these internal parts is hard. The heart,
At least, beats. The stomach sickens with a slick
Of bad milk. The lifelong quiet liver
Shivers finally at the whiskey's long shot.
Even the brain's decaying meat aches —
A butcher's cut one lugs from place to place.

But the mind discovers no way to break
Outside itself. "Nothing can come of nothing":
Tautology's small cell seals all too tight.
Of course, as in a fairy tale, there is a key
Just lying on the floor: three perfect,
Gilded syllables. It opens no door.

LEE PATTON

When Everything Is Goneril

what wouldn't you give for something Foolish,
for blazing double entendre and illuminating wit
as sharp as a servant's truth? What wouldn't you give
to weave a garland in your young daughter's hair
and spend the whole day under the wide sky
in a field where wildflowers beckon, unpicked?
Then, tired, giddy, all you'd yearn for's home.

But there stands Goneril: hospitality has claws,
duty's barbaric with ancient grievances, and
she does, after all, hold the deed by birth, by law.
Though love is often declaimed, it's really disowned,
houseless in this ungenerous land — sent to wander
in bald lots, sent to sleep under cardboard punctured
for a glimpse of smudged and savage stars.

MICHELLE LABARRE

For Gloucester on Being Newly Blind

I could have taught the actor a thing or two
about being led.
About being blind.

You are not groping with your chin
and your hand is not desperate to touch.
It is hoping
for an empty path.

Your eyes don't prefer to be closed,
they read the sound
of blackness.

Your first steps will be shy. They will ask
for details because there is risk
in picking your feet up
off the ground.
There are implications in the sandpaper
of concrete
and the garbled speech
of gravel.

Your foot will know negative space
by its silence;
in silence your mind may find shadows.

Your actor's body must cry the humiliation
of being led.
And your eyes must cry
the disappointment
of the light.

SHERYL CORNETT

Lear Expands His Last Words to Cordelia

Now you see it: the autumn of me
a stained-glass person backlit
by the setting sun which neither
warms these frail limbs nor
restores my once-thick
tenor to its elixir.

Now you see it: my life lowering
itself, dipping to the west and
disappearing into a night cloud
of unknowing. Death's distant
cousin drives away daylight's
angst into sleep, sweet sleep.

Now you see me: dying
consumed by loving
not wisely, not well, not others
much at all. Tell me, then, why I
stand here redeemed in late-hour
daughter-love, grown rich in grace.

CHARLES CLIFTON

Lear Drives His Rambler across Laurel Mountain

You read about the wreckage
up on Laurel Mountain. A strange
old man, wildflowers in his hair,
lost along the berm and babbling
about his kingdom and his daughters,
the lapsed insurance on his car,
little Cordelia sitting on his lap
to help him steer, the road
that led from where he thought
he was to where he was, the road
he thought he saw turning
above the tops of cabins
and telephone poles and clouds
that called to mind the castle
and leading directly into the shining
heart of the mystery of things. Ha.
For him an easy choice. He pops
her into second, and takes off.

In the old days his horse
might have been expected
to nose his mortal way back
to the sweet hay of his stable,
followed by the hoofbeats of a hundred.
But now Lear knows the game
adds up to nothing, a zero-
sum commodity, he is born
into our world a weeping infant,
no woman there to comfort him.
We wawl and cry. I will preach to thee.

The sky darkens. The light goes out.
We bend our heads toward Laurel Mountain,
imagining in the sound of the storm

some far-off catastrophe. In the morning
I pick apples off the ground, too bruised
and too sweet to eat, and chunk them
against the beat garage door. Then
comes the sharp voice of my mother —
"Stop playing and bring those apples in,
your poor old father's lost his job."

CECILIA WOLOCH

Ottava Rima: Lear

Perhaps we ought to be ashamed and aren't
of Daddy lying helpless in that room,
tethered to the bed, and frail and bent
who was God as in Our Father once but whom
we bathe like our own child and kiss and pet
and introduce to strangers we bring home
as if he still might rise up like a king —
white-haired, wild-eyed, fearless, welcoming.

KEN POBO

Stormy Lear

Every day at work I see suited
men, shoes shined,
professionalism a poison
odor they emit — lackey Lears
dividing up a kingdom
of ego.

They never come to work
in a hibiscus jockstrap
or a coat of many colored
dahlias. How sad they look!
How badly they need
a storm to rumple them,

make them get naked
and fall into a flower field.
They don't. They're kings
who rule — without mercy.

DAVID WRIGHT

Lines on Retirement, after Reading *Lear*

for Richard Pacholski

Avoid storms. And retirement parties.
You can't trust the sweetnesses your friends will
offer, when they really want your office,
which they'll redecorate. Beware the still
untested pension plan. Keep your keys. Ask
for more troops than you think you'll need. Listen
more to fools and less to colleagues. Love your
youngest child the most, regardless. Back to
storms: dress warm, take a friend, don't eat the grass,
don't stand near tall trees, and keep the yelling
down — the winds won't listen, and no one will
see you in the dark. It's too hard to hear
you over all the thunder. But you're not
Lear, except that we can't stop you from what
you've planned to do. In the end, no one leaves
the stage in character — we never see
the feather, the mirror held to our lips.
So don't wait for skies to crack with sun. Feel
the storm's sweet sting invade you to the skin,
the strange, sore comforts of the wind. Embrace
your children's ragged praise and that of friends.
Go ahead, take it off, take it all off.
Run naked into tempests. Weave flowers
into your hair. Bellow at cataracts.
If you dare, scream at the gods. Babble as
if you thought words could save. Drink rain like cold
beer. So much better than making theories.
We'd all come with you, laughing, if we could.

FLOYD SKLOOT

The Role of a Lifetime

I am bound
Upon a wheel of fire.... (4.7.45–46)

He could not imagine himself as Lear.
He could do age. He could rage on a heath.
Wounded pride, a man gone wild: he could be clear
on those, stalking the stage, ranting beneath
a moon tinged red. Let words rather than full-
throated roars carry fury while the wind
howled. He could do that. And the awful pull
of the lost daughter, the old man more sinned
against than sinning. The whole wheel of fire
thing. But not play a wayward mind! Be cut
to the brains, strange to himself, his entire
soul wrenched free, then remember his lines but
act forgetting. Understand pure nonsense
well enough to make no sense when saying
it. Wits turned was one thing; wits in absence
performed with wit was something else. Playing
Lear would force him to inhabit his fear,
fathom the future he had almost reached
already. Why, just last week, running here
and there to find lost keys, a friend's name leached
from memory. Gone. No, nor could he bring
himself to speak the plain and awful line
that shows the man within the shattered king:
I fear I am not in my perfect mind.

EDWIN ROMOND
Lady Macbeth, Afterward

Was it the ghoul in you that craved sex
after murder, that desired a husband
who trembled with another man's blood?
Or was it the corpse of a king,
a hallway away, daggered in his last dream,
that became your aphrodisiac? Outside,
owls stabbed at falcons and stallions
gnawed each other but, in bed, it was your hands
that had their way, forcing his face
to your breasts, leading him into you,
you, who bragged you had unsexed yourself,
even you became inflamed with what the living
live for. And afterward, when you exhaled
"I love you," he answered with crazed silence
as lightning flashed your windows
like eyes of a furious God.

LEE UPTON
The Ditch

The inside of the spine of *Macbeth* is ditch-dark.
I have been looking through these pages
    remembering
the knock at the door.

    Whoever takes a walk in the moonless night —
his head will be "stove-in."
    A storm.
I couldn't find what I was looking for.

    All this way! Coming down the stairs!
Into a cellar with dampening walls.
A hand for decades must have moved across
    the pages of this very book,

slowly, lower each time —
    too afraid to touch a head wound.
The spine is not entirely broken,
    yet here and there begins to fall back

as if weight through so many years
    pulled it apart
like an infant divided
    into two hands, into humanity.

STEVEN MARX

Mark Antony's Valentine

"You cannot call it love, for at your age,
The heyday of the blood is tame," said he —
An ignorant child who never could presage
What nature's secret of love's growth would be.
No less than air or food or sun's warm ray
Your sound, your smell, your taste, your touch, your sight
Still animate, sustain and calm the clay
That sinks into my mattress every night.
No less the rose of dawn, the bloom of spring
For being welcomed yet another time.
Appreciation of a precious thing
Accumulates before it turns sublime;
Even in depletion, more entire
And poignant, knowing soon it must expire.

ADRIANNE MARCUS
Cleopatra

So out of death, she breathes
him into life, a shadow
larger than the sun. She
is wrapped in cloth of gold
waiting on her barge.
This Antony is more than
Roman. He is her match.

Dolabella, still human, cannot
understand. Antony is dead.
She cannot hold him. And Rome
persists, belongs to Caesar.

But she is Cleopatra. Unrehearsed.
Alone. Darkness, rising from the
Nile, the shifting monuments
of sand. What does she
see or hear in all that unforgiving
blackness? Not Caesar, who has
won, nor even Antony, who is,
at last, like her: untouchable.

Whatever's there or absent
she must love. And so she turns
to absence, begins her journey
toward the place which will
extend to meet her. Easily
she fits the golden collar
to her throat. Then ebony,
amber, at each wrist. She is
smiling as she reaches up,
unbinds her dress.

Out of that long Egyptian night
she brings to her own death,

herself. In the final moments
before her chambered walls
dissolve, she sees it:
her barge, gleaming,
in the clear, unanchored night.

JIM PETERSON
As If

The dream in which I was Shakespeare . . .
— a friend

When I was Shakespeare,
the weight of a new manuscript under my arm
bound and tied with leather
was enough to sustain the fight in me.
And my hands, which wanted nothing more
than to turn the pockets of strangers inside out,
curled up like fists even when I slept.

When I was Shakespeare, the moon
etched my face on the windowpane,
the sun carved my shadow in the dust
and the dogs abandoned by the dead
could not obliterate it.
The critics who sat in the galleries,
who never felt the rain on their heads
in the midst of soliloquy,
who never tasted the cold roots of originality
bitter and foreboding in their mouths,
scribbled their tiny paragraphs, their palsied puns,
then avoided my eyes later in the pub
as if I ever gave a good god damn.

PART IV *Hamlet*

JAMES APPLEWHITE

On the Mississippi

"Ophelia: Ope not thy ponderous and marble
      jaws," said the Duke on the raft,
adrift, forgetful, among yawning people,
          Arkansas-miles from his craft.

The cloud of a war, that hadn't happened yet,
      hung over Huck and Jim, as they overheard
the young fraud tell the old how to play Hamlet —
        project that would get them tarred

and feathered, eventually. The mighty bard
      fell mute among ignorant innocents, till the folk
they'd coaxed from woodlot and hut with word
        of the Royal Nonesuch saw a joke

they could get — naked, striped man as speech
      for such wilderness. The river Twain knew
graphs the distance the Dane has to reach
        toward us, Old Worlders new

to the silence of landscape — swallowed whole
      by it, as once nearly Ishmael.
Remembering, we falter, our jaws grow ponderous, almost
        Ophelia's. With lips for the lost.

PETER MEINKE

Noreen

In any group there are the beautiful and
the plain the strong & weak smart as a trinket
& dumb as a clam Agreed But there's little
agreement who they are or correlation
with how they all turn out Noreen here lying

on the storeroom floor with her head on a sack
of potatoes phone dangling from the wall and
a plastic cup of vodka on the shelf was
voted Wittiest in the Class and the Girl
with the Nicest Eyes *Where be your gibes now?* asked

Hamlet as indeed did Noreen when playing
Hamlet in ninth grade pronouncing it *guybs* while
Miss Endicott rolled her eyes which weren't half
as nice as Noreen's Outside it's been dead cold
and rainy for a month and polluted air

gums your glasses like snails the ink smears on her
lover's letter *Dear Noreen* For years she has
held the wrong job the wrong man She even had
the wrong child Those are the reasons How much we
need reasons! How reasons make us feel better!

ALICE FRIMAN

Diapers for My Father

Pads or pull-ons — *that*
is the question. Whether to buy
pads dangled from straps
fastened with buttons or Velcro —
pads rising like a bully's cup
stiff as pommel with stickum backs
to stick in briefs. Or, dear God,
the whole thing rubberized,
size 38 in apple green, with
or without elastic leg. Or the kind,
I swear, with an inside pocket
to tuck a penis in — little resume
in a folder. Old mole, weeping
his one eye out at the tunnel's end.

The clerk is nothing but patience
practiced with sympathy.
Her eyes soak up everything.
In ten minutes she's my cotton batting,
my triple panel, triple shield — my Depends
against the hour of the mop: skeleton
with a sponge mouth dry as a grinning brick
waiting in the closet.

She carries my choices to the register,
sighing the floor with each step.
I follow, absorbed away to nothing.

How could Hamlet know what flesh is heir to?
Ask Claudius, panicky in his theft,
hiding in the garden where it all began
or behind the arras, stuffing furbelows
from Gertrude's old court dress into his codpiece.
Or better, ask Ophelia, daughter too
of a foolish, mean-mouthed father,
who launched herself like a boat of blotters
only to be pulled babbling under the runaway stream.

SANDY FEINSTEIN

Tendered

My father never sweat
through heavy cotton
clothing as he counted
conquests, nameless
in war and rented rooms.
He broke virgins,
my mother,
knowing like Polonius
how men tender girls
like treasure
spent.

Hamlet's poetry
is naked enough
that he may come
fully dressed to bed
and wait
for Ophelia
to breathe desire
like a hand in the dark
seeking for something
only daughters
want.

MARVIN BELL

Sounds of the Resurrected Dead Man's Footsteps (#1)

1. *Baby Hamlet*

Be that as it may, it may be that it is as it will be.
His word a sword without a hiss.
Cruelly, the son obliged to sacrifice himself to a feud.
On the Feast of the Angel of Consumption and Death.
We move through time beset by indecision.
Thus, events occur while waiting for the news.
Or stuck in moral neutral.
The Nazis willing to let aid enter the camps if those bringing it swore not
    to help the prisoners escape.
The hopeless pacifism of those who promised.
The Platonic ideal carried to its logical inconclusion.
The heroes those who lied to the Third Reich.
Otherwise, the world stands caught between Hamlet and Ophelia.
Ophelia's dress a dead ringer for beauty.

2. *The Play within the Play*

Hamlet a man asked to die now.
Madness to try to make sense of a father's ghost.
To know one lives yet may not.
To imbibe a poison over time — wishing to be, yet consigned.
And the work details, the meager rations, the Motherland.
Destined to clog the machinery of the State with one's body, Nazis the mas-
    ters of whitewash.
Fairy dust rising from lime shoveled into the grave.
Poems and postmortems a struggle with Danish collaboration.
Hamlet a play of ones foreshadowing a time of millions.
Hamlet addressing a skull the poet speaking to the dead.
Bones the bloodless gray of ancient manuscripts.
The eyes marbles clicking in their pockets.
Hamlet done to death with his head in his hands.

PETER COOLEY

For Hamlet

All afternoon: the rain, monotonous, my prison bars.
This room, the monotony of my body, spirit up against it,

cells within the cell. How is it once
I had to call to you who daily now appear

wrapped in dark clouds, storming my study's view
upon the backyard, to soliloquize and brood,

utterly unasked for? Now you are here, ranting,
the black sun rising as melancholy locks me up

inside a moment I cannot move beyond.
Hamlet, I am sentenced to you, whom I hoped

after my youth to break out of, to be
as other men, outgrowing your indecisions,

vatic and manic, for the world of business
paved with busyness, reorganized each morning.

Now I am too long melancholy, fifty-three,
to shake off these poles in which I vacillate

unable to take hold, seize, articulate
even my love to three children or a wife

without some swoon or rage or savage quip
which answers to the name of action. I would banish

you to a foreign country under false pretense
did I not know I would flee myself

in that self-same breath. Hush, brother,
the rain begins to fall more softly

hearing me confessing this. Now you can sleep.
I'll keep the watch all night if need be for your sake.

We have the ghosts of more than fathers between us, stalking.

MAURYA SIMON

Helsinore, Denmark

September 25, 2000

We looked for your ghosts here, Hamlet,
but all that we found finally, at day's close,
was dusk's self-guided tour of the dungeons.

We meandered dark corridors underground,
my husband and I, my raincoat dragging
across the floor like Ophelia's drowned hair.

Little battered bulbs wanly sparked at us
from the stony walls that led us past roomy
catacombs where, when we entered on tiptoe,

the cloistered dark sent shivers down our necks,
for that emptiness seemed brusquely human.
Finally the dim-lit trail petered out into a space

reeking of rotting fish: I nearly swooned —
so we rushed back up to open air, blinking,
and no one around to explain why those vats

made of granite housed gallons of putrid fins
and scales, those awful, rancid coffers of fish —
and you, poor Prince, where was your ghost?

In the silent, lilac gloom, I saw only a mouse
limping like a drunken sentry across the cold
and cobbled courtyard towards the drawbridge,

turning his head back to us just once, briefly,
as if to ascertain whether we, too, had issued
from some deep cavern of the mind, or whether

we might, instead, have come back from the dead
like Polonius, to proffer him the barest crumb
of kindness, a clouded-over fish's eye.

MARJORIE MADDOX
Cancer Diagnosis

I. O

Words cage heart and breath,
irregular in trepidation.
Where are the open arms of hope?
This oval of prognostication
clamps prayer, interrogates pulse.
Even a howl echoes
within its ribs.

II. *that this too too sullied flesh*

Skin-deep and rank,
righteousness flees these organs
ripe with mortality's regret.
Wishes are hollow bones.
Even a Faustian switch
cannot remix the obvious.

III. *would melt, thaw*

Soon disease dissolves all self,
liquidates the I.
Listen for the drip of solitude
and relent. The dark waters
of doubt ebb and flow too quickly
downstream.

IV. *and resolve itself into a dew*

Not dust but drops
about to evaporate in sun,
to rise in the heat of forgiveness,
this strange healing that peels
skin from soul, sanctifying what rots
and is rotten in the state
of who we are.

LEON STOKESBURY

Reynaldo in Paris

"Ooo-la-la!" remarked Reynaldo. "Tonight
my wick shall dip in ecstasies once more
as I plunge deeper through that nunnery door,
Miss Mimi's house of sale, then jam it tight.
Back home, I smelled the rotten fault all right,
so took the bucks and split from that dumb bore
and got out while the gettin' was good, before
shit hit the fan and blotted out the light.

What wine so sweet as little Mimi's seat!
Now that's the song I'm singing every day.
So let them grab each other by the balls.
For what care I whose slick, incestuous meat
gets gnawed between those sheets? And what care they
for fardel-bearing sots who play their thralls?"

R. S. GWYNN

Horatio's Philosophy

Absented from felicity a year
In the back room let by his maiden aunts,
He let his hair grow long and pierced one ear,
Staring at cards Reynaldo mailed from France.

The scenes which they depicted gave him pause.
Stranger than Pliny (he had flunked the course),
In violation of all natural laws
A lady copulated with a horse.

If such as that could be, how stale and flat
Would seem the stupid tale he'd sworn to write:
The spider nesting in the old king's hat,
The late appearance of the northern lights,

Simple adultery and the rancid stew
Which he'd passed on but cost the crown its life,
His fat friend's garter tangling with his shoe,
Pitching him forward on his letter-knife,

And worse, that senile windbag and his daughter,
The former shafted with a curtain rod,
The latter diving into six-inch water.
This was the stuff of tragedy? Dear God.

The memo came from Osric, now the Chief
Of Royal Information: *Get to work!*
Keep the thing scandalous, and keep it brief.
Action and jokes. Make everyone a jerk

Except, of course, King Fortinbras. Let him
(Deus ex machina) arrive in time
To get lard-ass's blessing. You can trim
Most of the facts. Put in some crime

To make us look legitimate. And need
I mention that you've missed your deadline — twice?
Next week. At latest. Then, as we agreed,
You'd best get out of town. Take my advice.

And so he sat there hours, thinking hard.
Paris? Why not? But he was tired and broke
And known by face to every border guard.
The truth was bad enough. This was a joke.

His skills, such as they were, lay in debating
Questions of ethics, and his style of prose
Would never keep the groundlings salivating
With prurient puns. He'd seen Lord Osric's shows.

But what was truth? Wasn't it, all things said,
Whatever the authorities deemed right?
The rest was silence, for the dead were dead.
Feeling much better, he began to write.

The first draft took two days. He hired a ghost,
Dictating while he packed and paced the floor.
By Friday he had made it to the coast,
Sunday, stood knocking at Reynaldo's door.

NAN COHEN

Horatio

I do not know from what part of the world
I should be greeted, if not from Lord Hamlet. (4.6.5–6)

The direct stare will get you exactly nowhere
with the supporting character. First, he's not looking at you.
Student of archaeology,
he sifts the layers represented in the castle;
he divines the origin of each sentimental knickknack's
placement on an occasional table, he understands
the mat and doily on the piano, the subtle geography
of Louis Seize, Queen Anne, Arabia, Delft
accumulated in various regimes, the tectonic shifts
of braces of photographs, portraits groaning on the walls —

but always he looks back to the prince, to catch the very eye
of fury and confusion, as if the shouts, the crashing into chairs,
the whispers and popping of knuckles were a language
he might learn, or at least make into sense,
given enough time and his accomplished diligence.
Study makes the scholar a stranger to his home —

so don't look at him. Take as read
the faithful friend, and instead look where he's looking.

Student of astronomy,
he knows some things can be seen with the averted glance:
color lives in the center of the eye (a man slips
behind a purple curtain; a distraught girl
in draggled lace and grass stains
hovers at the hem of the audience, sighing)
but black and white thrive on the verge —

he thinks of Andromeda's velvet
drapery, the other galaxy
that hides behind her skirts, that only appears,

like a flaw in a lens, when you look askew.
Safer that way.

Look at Horatio, and you'll see his friend the prince.
But stare at the prince, and you'll see his galaxy's
peculiar movement around him,
his starts and jags, beyond the power
of a friend's equations to describe.

Student of literature,
he knows the poet's trick of examining
the sagging porch in lieu of the fight with the wife,
the bauble to talk about Beauty, all the old dodges and feints.
He himself is not a metaphor;
he can't say what he came here for.

RICHARD HEDDERMAN

The First Player's Monologue

We will use all gently, my lord,
even the darkness that englobes
the fluttering soul of each candle.
We will wait for your signal —
standing on a coffin lid,
sawing the air with both your hands
— and begin at the raven's first,
querulous cry, long after twilight
has cleared the ramparts. Soon,
we will find ourselves once again
in the garden, where sooner or later
we all come to ruin, and will orchestrate
your disharmony: this play about poison
and torches, the malevolence of power
and the evil of gardens.
We will show how he died, your ghost:
where the sunflower nodded in perpetuity,
where a root slept, and a tree
burnt in the sunlight; where a heart stopped.
I, too, will be nervous
as I approach the sleeper
and the ear, that cauldron of suspicion,
fluting inward and mirroring the labyrinth
of the soul. We will do it so the king
will recognize himself,
even in the smoky light
of the tapers, and shudder. Observe!
If he twitches like a fly, or leaps up
in a flurry of gestures!
The torches will dim, if only for a moment,
silks will rustle and tapestries whisper
in the sudden, incandescent quiet.
Hair will bristle at the touch of horror.
We will remain still and let death

take its stance among the groundlings
of this rotten state.
Your father will hear
the oboes stop as the cries
of the guilty unearth him,
the last note lingering
on the liquid porches of the ear.
And the next time you see the ghost,
have him breathe on a mirror
and prove his shape; death
is just the absence of time.
The rest is silence.

DAVID OLIVEIRA

Laurence Olivier's Hamlet

He is 41, his mother 28. Blonder than Denmark, there isn't enough dye
in the bottle to turn him into a schoolboy. Sweet prince of the theater
before the movies, he has a taste for lace cuffs and intricate embroidery,
but dons simple tights in every scene — fittingly black for mourning a father.

It's the classic story: The father too preoccupied with work to notice that
his bored wife is occupied by his younger brother. Indifferent to the family
business, the overprotected son parties away at college, perennially shy
of graduation credits. When his father dies unexpectedly, the son, victim
of chronic vacillation (he has yet to figure out what his major is going to be
or not to be), can't decide how best to get home — missing Father's funeral,
Mother's wedding, and the coveted crown (he's first runner-up). Not the
only son to ever face the ghost of a father, he doesn't handle the situation
well — wanting nothing more than to curl up on Mother's busy bed.

Trim enough for the stage, the plot sheds two hours to fit into the movies.
Rosencrantz and Guildenstern are gone before they can be killed, something
everyone regrets. Olivier and Alan Dent share writing credit — mentioned
is the aspiring author of the effusive first draft (unavailable for the rewrite).
For Sir Larry, who directs himself, it's all black and white — just the simple
"tragedy of a man who couldn't make up his mind."

Snow and the Academy Awards fall on the first day of spring in L.A., 1949.
Their gowns under wraps, actresses and heels slip through Hollywood's
icy streets more easily than usual. The great Ethel B., who has been in all
the papers for weeks touting her brother John's greater Dane, presents
the award for Best Picture — the winner's name trippingly on the tongue.
The writing, which seems to some derivative and clichéd, isn't nominated.
In London to do a play with wife, Vivien, Olivier celebrates with an extra
drink after the show — as do the losers. This night he has a bit of trouble
falling asleep, his head reeling in words — sublime, unforgettable words.

J. KATES

Nothing in Art

> *Boy, nothing in art talks like a human skull.*
> — Randall Jarrell

Clacking my teeth only when you are here
to clack them for me, speaking ironic lines
only through Shakespeare's art and Hamlet's scope,
paperweight on the sill of Saint Jerome,
I am a prop, an object for your posing;
how can you mock my nakedness by saying

I carry on as if I were unique?
You use me willfully and when you're done
you throw me in a corner of the trunk
knowing my only virtue is the strength
of mute and simple matter — if I crack,
so much the better for your meditation.

Don't get me wrong: I have no complaints.
Don't try to read anything into me.
Whatever you are, you are. Don't try to hide
behind my grin; there are no one-way mirrors.
Look to the mirrors of your own strong hands;
feel the flesh of your face, the weight within;

leap with imagination through the wall
I raise against your touch; look out, look out
and feel the thread of nerve from here to there.
These words are written down by flesh and mind,
read them with mind and flesh, and hear the blood
pounding against the inside of your head.

GAIL WHITE

Queen Gertrude's Soliloquy

I wish he wouldn't sulk, it's unbecoming,
and first impressions ought to be our best.
Then I do wish he'd stop that beastly humming
and talking to himself. "Give it a rest —
you're acting out!" I long to say, but no,
a mother can't, that's being interfering.
Of course he was at school, and ought to go
again, but Claudius gets hard of hearing
if I bring that up. As for other means —
Ophelia? She's a darling, but not quite
the sort of character one wants in queens —
all sugar and no spice. She'd never fight
his weaknesses. Old friends? I'll take the chance!
I'll send for Guildenstern and Rosencrantz.

LEE UPTON
Gertrude to Hamlet

Inside, the turned liver,
the shiny capsules,
the taffeta

bladders and envelopes.
Would you divide
the anatomical

destinies of a heart?
I have no business
that is not a functioning

mystery to you,
a blooming peony
and a purse of tears.

Dust, ash
or nothingness,
what tears

in bursting waves,
ill-tempered stresses.
Say what you please

I am
up to my hands
in a split creature.

Which makes my body my own.
I live in it, I gather
my own into it. Otherwise,

who would you be,
beginning to be?
You wander my throne like measles.

D. C. BERRY

Hambone Two Tongue

I'm what you might call a two-track Hamster,
twirl the treadmill opposite ways at once —
double-talk Ham — like telling the players,
"Don't rant and rave like pro-wrestling bozos,"
then ask for the opposite, a melodrama
of raving pro-wrestling bombastic rant.
The ham with two tongues, me — with one tongue, I
tell the clowns don't add your jokes to the play,
then with my other tongue, I make up skits
with any jumping bean who comes along
and end up ignoring the ghost's hot script
to make the play a spaghetti thrilla.
I double-talk the ear off my best friend:
I swear to Horatio that I don't flatter,
then candy him to spy on Claudius.
Merry-go-round I go, two ways at once:
chew myself out, then turn around and yawn,
my words more gilt on Claudius' crown.

KEVIN GRIFFITH

Hamlet Meets Frankenstein

For Frankenstein, of course, Hamlet's central
problem is irrelevant. The monster
offs the king in the first act,
dispatches Polonius quickly with a twist
of the neck, and then terrorizes the kingdom
until he ascends to the throne,
a feared leader, making the phrase
"There's something rotten in Denmark"
his badge of honor, an official seal.
Ophelia is fished from the river,
brought back to life with a bolt of lightning
and made his bride, a fitting queen.

Meanwhile, Hamlet is still sulking
at the grave site, skull in hand
and three dead kings to contend with,
one still very much in charge.
Remarkably, the play ends like all tragedies:
The dead watch over the living,

and the living wonder why it's so hard to be alive.

JACK CONWAY

This Is What Happens When You Let Hamlet Play Quarterback

Sure he can sling that ball
downfield like an arrow,
but he keeps calling the same play
in the huddle.

Before the snap,
he's looking in the stands for his father
and wishes his mother would act her age
and quit the cheerleading squad.

RYAN G. VAN CLEAVE

Hamlet at the Paris Aerobleu

He's working the alto saxophone
like Ella Fitzgerald does an ankle-long
cocktail dress of spun gold — what else

would a prince play but the sax,
that cindercone stick that knows
all seven steps to heaven?

Hamlet sips his highball, then howls
through his horn in that basic black voice
all men learn when they harmonize

with death, lost double octaves throbbing
in the air like a broken circuit, the electricity
still there, spinning like Wes Montgomery

on a turntable, always cooking.
Max Morgan, a momentary silhouette
against the bar's rhinestone skin,

lights a cigarette. Everywhere, the agony
of an impossible flight of notes, a black hole
that bores into every soul, flaunting power, pain.

PETER CUMMINGS

Hamlet to Ophelia

Doubt thou the stars are fire,
Doubt that the sun doth move,
Doubt truth to be a liar,
But never doubt I love. (2.2.116–19)

If I could speak with you . . . but that's all gone,
since we by fathers are in that forbid,
I could assure you of what has been done,
or what I think my "uncle-father" did.
But I can't speak (or even send) this verse,
since walls have ears and corridors have eyes,
and doubt's a growing cancer of a curse
that multiplies in hiring new spies.
The mind's a second-guesser of the truth,
and in its labyrinths will find a way
to weasel past the fact, that most uncouth
of players in the life we daily play.
    I love you. Or at least I think I love,
    but that's a theory that's still left to prove.

ALLISON JOSEPH

Not Ophelia

I don't have golden hair to toss around,
my eyes aren't pools of blue to sing about.
Don't tell me I'm the angel that you've found
to send you floating high, free from doubt.

My eyes aren't pools of blue to sing about;
I'm not diaphanous or delicate —
to send you floating high, free from doubt.
Don't talk of "thee" and "thou" — you need to wait.

I'm not diaphanous or delicate —
I'm clumsy as they come, my life in shards.
Don't talk of "thee" and "thou" — you need to wait,
find someone else's "essence" — those discards.

I'm clumsy as they come, my life in shards;
don't tell me I'm the angel that you've found.
Find someone else's essence, those discards.
I don't have golden hair to toss around.

WILLIAM GREENWAY

Ophelia Writes Home

He passed so peacefully in sleep, it seemed
as in a kingly way, or in at least
what passes for a royal death in this
rough place where every bush may hide a bear.
He was a good provider, and we lived
if not as kings, then as two princes who
were born to make the best of baser things
and not forget how blessed we were to be
alive at all. It was Horatio,
you now can know, who hatched the plan to bate
the sword with sleeping potion, culled from stuff
he'd read at school in Wittenberg about
the young Italian lovers, feuding tribes,
a tomb for two. It just remained to bribe
the graveyard clowns to feign and shuttle both
the boxes (I no longer shivering
and wet) on board the pirate ship we dubbed
The Nunnery, a little jest which fed
the joy we felt in one another's arms
across the icy sea, until we reached
this Eden Danish men discovered past
the coldest land of all. Our children grew,
the crops rose tall, the swarthy neighbors brought
their harvest in to honor us at fall.
This is in secret — should you draw your breath
to tell his tale do not this letter show,
thereby his famous tragedy amending.
Recall his melancholy cast and know
how much he would abhor a happy ending.

KATHLEEN LYNCH
Ophelia in Utah

I lay down singing, down
in the glassy stream, my arms
laden with crow-flowers, nettles,
my mouth still telling prayer
and songs of grief, my mind,
they say, gone. O father,
brother, lover, those heavy
skirts and what I carried
bore me down, and under
the green water I left you,
left you my body to plant.
Imagine my surprise
when not just time passed
but all space and dimension,
and I surfaced farther away
than you or I could ever imagine.
This is a lake of salt, where all tears
come to rest, and I am buoyant here,
bare under a very bare sky, completely
awake now, and curious. I carry nothing
but words. What have they named
the flowers in this windblown place?
Who will I meet if I rise up, walk
to the far road? I will say *Here I am.*
I will wear the one face God gave me.
The water is a vast breathing thing,
it grows dark beneath me, dark
and deeper still.

TRACY S. YOUNGBLOM

Ophelia Speaks

They always had me
and my tongue.

Now I see my own speech
spread like a tapestry
across the knees
of this silence. I have time
to study its threads,
pluck at the errant ones.
I'm warming to the task.

I only repeated what I was told.
It was true, I thought nothing.
But the prayers,
those were mine, cast up
to shatter the glass of heaven,
coarsen the ground
on which I walked
with its broken shards.
Unhallowed ground, that's what
you call it.

Then I went mad and found
I could speak. Madness found me,
and I spoke. They let me
speak — sing — standing there,
dumb. And her looking up
for help, the *beauteous majesty*
of nothing. And nothing
looking back.
The nothing I made.

RICHARD HEDDERMAN
Ophelia

Under spring stars,
he touched my face and breasts,
and the innumerable moons of my body.

For months, I listened for him
everywhere, hearing his laugh now and again
down stone corridors, or across the hushed drifts
that chilled Elsinore.

And once only did I find him,
that shadow darkening his strange brow,
talking to the players in whispers
in some cold chamber.

My refuge, then, was the childhood willow
where I climbed and sang clear
above the brook.

And when I descended into the arms
of the water, I turned slowly
listening with eyelashes, fingertips,
one arm thrown wide to the current
that swallowed me like snow.

LEILANI HALL

Ophelia's Rant before She's Heavy with Drink

I speak like a green girl,
wear my dress as a turned asphodel,
the petals white, fallen in shards at my ankles.
Don't follow me; my own feet already bleed,
having trailed Hamlet loosed out of hell,
offered him quince, access
to the blossoms you had me deny.
You said declension, into the madness wherein
now he raves, as if those murky caves
he walks in his mind were both star and abyss,
anyplace out of my reach.
But these arms are as long as the willow branches
bent and pouting into the creek, the small chubs
spawning and reckless. I may not know how to wreck
less, how to undo stockings down-gyved, distressed
as I have been to keep any terrible bird from the honey
of Hamlet's vows. Naïve as you say I am, I may still weave
garlands — dead-nettle, crow-flowers. I can do this numb,
unconscious of my hands, the snap of limbs,
babble of water.

KIRSTEN DIERKING
Delacroix's Version

Ophelia hangs still tangible
in a pool so green it drifts

between a languid peace and a
dead calm. She is holding onto

a branch, her mouth passive,
but well above her liquid line

of obligation. Maybe she'll
float for one afternoon, drag

herself out, but this is only
a dream, unframed. The branch

she is holding is not even
as thick as her arm. Her hair

is already weaving in weeds,
her dress is draped serenely

with sleep. Even the tree's
critical limbs are cracking now,

urging her to accept her immersion,
while she is still lovely,

surrendering.

RYAN G. VAN CLEAVE

Ophelia on a Graveled Garden Walk in Purgatory

The rarest commodity here is color —
even the flowers glisten with ill intent,
shapeless white specimens that bake
under a sunless sky, their dying stink
gummed into the grass, the cloudless air.

Ophelia rushes past the peonies, torn
to pieces by people gone choleric
for a speck of butterfly purple, a stripe
of flyrod black. But Ophelia does not
care because she is alone in true misery,

her heart still full and kicking like a green
horse — the others are siphoned of spirit,
the drabbest ones male, the females vulgar
wisps who speak in voices scored with frost.
She traces dust lines in the path, watches

whitecaps in the distance, wondering all
the while if the ponds at Elsinore are clear
of ice, if H is kneeling there, face lifted
to the sun, as his heart soars, a duck
lifting slow from a stand of dark reeds.

SUSAN TERRIS
Ophelia

> *You speak like a green girl,*
> *Unsifted in such perilous circumstance.* (1.3.101–02)

She woke to a mockingbird and sensed a lucky day.
Face decaled against panes, she browsed
the morning. Unjacketed, she flung herself past
blue door and gate, skinked across the grass
to where he lay coiled, waiting.
Unsifted, she offered rosemary, pansies. Unsifted,
she exulted when hair tangled to silken knots and
stockings pleated at her ankles. *I love you,* she
breathed, then breathed it again, thirsty for
his reply. But as he rolled her
in grass cuttings, she felt tiny sharpened spears
prick, draining away green, fading all to brown.

REGINALD SHEPHERD

Snowdrops and Summer Snowflakes, Drooping

The river is silted with sentiments, Ophelia
sings flowers in hell to all the goodnight
ladies martyred to plot, rosemary, pansies, fennel
and rue, columbine, wormwood and oxeyed daisies:
wilting litanies of no consequence. She scatters
handfuls of snow in no tense, returning
to the same spot she brings her spotless
suffering, called Candor, or Covert.

I'd give her trillium and yarrow, wild
carrot or white sweet clover,
some roadside blossoms less
historical: invasive wood sorrel, dame's
rocket, handfuls of designations,
names of names; stems broken, weeping
sap to sting her fingers, draw the flies,
make her drop her bottle of virginity.

I'd give her brambly honeysuckle
and dogwood bushes to shred her
wedding dress in passing to a proper
shroud, a weed or three to stain her white
with theirs, goodnight sweet lady,
wake up. What I wouldn't give
to hear her shut up that infernal singing,
walk out of sullen water open-eyed.

JUDITH H. MONTGOMERY

Ophelia, in Winter

Twisting out of fevered sheets,
she presses her blush heat and dark

against the windowpane to witness
winter's unsullied flurry, midnight snow caught

on lilac twigs, vesting brook and rock.
Beyond the glass, ink strokes of stubble

pierce the undulating body of the fields.
If she slipped through her reflection, she could drift

down the feathered path from which no one
could summon, no one take her. She tips

back her head, receives the chilled wafer
on her tongue. Kneels to watch her other face

ripple silver in black water. Lifts the chalice
to her lips, lets herself sink trackless

through white rapture. She becomes concealed —
as the knot coils in the pine,

as seeded grass genuflects in snow —
erasing the cloven print that bids the buck's

thighs to her melting source. She takes
that blue-tinged veil to cancel heat. Appetite.

ALICE FRIMAN

Ophelia

That Sunday nothing big moved.
Only flies. Ticks. Beetles.
Things that nibble and saw.
Gnats flying in hosts.
Dragonflies who dip a double wing
then drop to hover and watch.

All Elsinore. The cows.
The ghost. The rest. Heavy with heat.
Why else would she choose
water for her sleep?

She lay down easy, easy
as leaning back on a castle's
secret wall. She wasn't afraid.
Around her beetles walked on water,
coupling like saints to their own image
then gathered to her side
to twirl like dervishes
on the cool reflection of her sheets.
She floated, drifting and turning —
an abandoned boat, dripping
rings from her fingers. Her hair
unbraiding, spreading out like weed.

The sun flashed an SOS.
But she, half in half out,
surrendered to that wet cloister
the sound of her own heart held safe
in the wimple of water around her face.
She and her reflection consummated at last
in the lapping of that nunnery.

She leaned back into the water
as one presses into the side of sleep,

then turned her head
to kiss herself good night.

The dragonflies watched,
twisting their pea-green heads,
zoomed down on double wings
to pick and pluck their feed.
One lit on the bodice of her dress
and preened. Overhead, an oriole
flashed his beauty to hold her.

Under her, the water tilted
and swung open.

KIRSTEN KASCHOCK
As Birds in Rain

Ophelia had gathering hands and yet he was lost to her.
She opened the folds of her skirts and flew in water.
It rained that day.
Birds hid underwing as if to mourn.

The place by the river was a torn place. Rosemary. Rue.
Rain clung to her last scatterings as daughters, some daughters,
hold to their fathers in death. No bird flew from her.

The girl, pulled from the swollen river:
her hair, strangling her with leaves, her wet white gown.
All, all betrayed her.

The open fold of the grave was the last door. Birds
followed her down, and hid underwing, as if from rain,
and were covered with earth.

LEE MCCARTHY

Running Loose around the Castle

The grass skirt on the willow is yellow this morning.
Just above a shallow pool,
the long, flowing skirt of Ophelia sways in the wind,

pale yellow the right color for a young girl.
She's poor enough now her daddy's dead.
Shining through the tattered skirt is the flesh of sunlight.

Her mind having snapped some time ago,
she recites the limericks of herbs. Legs,
paler than even these leaves, twirl on feet

I cannot possibly see from this window
although I'm sure she's out there
barefoot in December.

ELON G. EIDENIER
The Failure of Language

She uttered what was lodged
within her heart, that desperate

need to share another body's warmth.
Ophelia's touch might have melted

Hamlet's cold suspicion, but love
could not wrap round her words,

carry them home to quilt his thoughts,
straighten the corridors of his mind.

Here is the failure of language:
words shifting from what is meant

to what is thought, to what is surmised;
unraveling all the sinews of care.

A stream-shroud covers her and sorrow
lifts her body just above the stones.

MICHAEL B. STILLMAN
Ophelia

Your lover held you
by the throat, still

you sang
like a swan.

The arrow falls as it must, bringing
down to the tremulous

pulse of the feathers
as they flutter almost
aimlessly

one final plume.

Let the wind spread tufts of milkweed
across the rippling surface of the brook

to mark the place
you fall, you

stain
the inevitable color
of your father's blood.

Your mind descends through currents it has found, refines
suffering
which would clarify
beyond song

all endings and all beginnings.

The flowing spring lay opening, deepening
when you died

among long purples.

SYLVIA ADAMS
Shakespeare's Eyebrows

When children are dying all around you
in Somalia, Srebrenica, your living room
it's comforting to know that Shakespeare's
eyebrows have been found, embedded in the
plaster cast of his death mask —
almost 400 years and most of us
didn't know they were missing.
Shakespeare himself didn't feel a thing, never
uttered a pox on the careless moulder.
Launched into the next world
sans eyebrows, he was well past the stage
of writing woeful ballads to a mistress;
had no fetish, brow or otherwise,
no time to measure shrunken shanks
or muse on which act had cut him short,
whether or not he was cheated out of
that last scene of all

And you, bit player, creeping in petty pace
as your tomorrows overtake and dwindle,
can pause to ponder future revelations:
a moustache whisker or flake of dandruff,
some poetic hem to touch and make you whole
articulate and free

This is as close as you will ever get
to love, these cold ends of dying
where you no longer impose conditions,
raise an eyebrow, perplexed or wounded
at a loved one's words or acts
or strain to choose the cruelest form of exit

PART V *The Romances*

ALFRED CORN

Reading *Pericles* in New London

The driven are the only ones to read
In cars; and double that for a patched-up thing
Like *The Prince of Tyre.* We've rolled to a standstill here,
A town that knew at least this much about us:
We'd need some classic service station, like Gulf
Or Mobil Oil . . . whose tricolor properties
These are: signs, pumps, uniforms,
All red-white-and-blue. (No stars or stripes, though.)
Throttles gun up and down; my nose crinkles
At the vibrant stench of fuel tainting the air;
And billboards across the way are advertising —
The Mystic Marina! (Jokes, coincidence,
And anachronism, the stuff of dreams and plays. . . .)
This Prologue says, "The older a good thing, the better."
Which doesn't quite account for classics, texts
A few dedicated bookworms devour,
Otherwise enshrined in gilt-edged neglect.
What makes me keep on turning pages and not
Just grunt, The End — I mean, since protest nudges
And says, Don't miss the goings-on around you.
Might be stubbornness; as well as glimmers
That I, not Shakespeare's play, am being judged.
(It would be different if we called to witness
His finest plays — *The Tempest, Hamlet, Lear* —
Which do, we feel, still sound contemporary
Depths.) I wonder what the Soul of the Age
Would make of New London. Would he think our brash,
If aging new world, El Dorado on wheels,
Stood on a plane with the old, a proper stage
For acts of global import framed in speech?
Well, everywhere you turn there are "characters";
And snatches of salty talk, some with a faint
Shakespearean ring — like this man's here, who grins
And takes a credit card as sunlight gilds
His hands. The chance for high-octane lines

Is to fuel many vehicles, deluxe
And budget compact both. Stately psalms,
You couldn't know you'd end up here as proverbs,
Of the party with drabs and scrapes of times
You never dreamed. . . . Indeed the truest author
Will put little credit in a captive future,
Betraying his age by having none, and all
Of them at once. Now first, now second, now
Third — a different gear for every scene,
Up to the last. Mystic Marina, be
Our oracle. The dolphin sometimes swims
In oil-stained seas; is it less delphic then?

REGINALD SHEPHERD

Pericles, Prince of Tyre: A Commentary

for Michael Dobson, onlie instigator

I

What makes a man? Ruby, carbuncle, beryl
and sard, all the purple dye in Tyre;
jasper, sunstone, chalcedony, the blood
-red carnelian. What makes a man the answer

to a riddle locked in a jeweled box? Find him
at home in storms (*he puts on sackcloth
and to sea*), backdrop of stitched cloudbanks
and paste gems cast into a cardboard surge

while Gower plays a red guitar.

What man marries a casket drowned at sea
and dedicates it to Diana? *Convey thy Deity
aboard our dancing boat.* Behold our hero, Pericles.
The moon exerts its pull on his unshaven hair,

his wave-lost head: steers him to Tarsus
and Pentapolis, Mytilene and Ephesus, a wayward tide
lashing the coast of Asia Minor. Great is Diana
descending from the ceiling in a gilded cage

when Gower plays his red guitar.

Someone has come to rob Marina of her maiden's jewel
and make himself a man of means. Another man
comes by her at a gallant price, and buys himself
a crown of gold, studded with garnet cabochons

and the signet of a full-blown sail, the canvas swell
mastered by song. She is a woman not of any shores,
where she was never born. *Thou art a man, and I
Have suffered like a girl. The gods make her prosperous*

though Gower plays a red guitar.

Some men marry their daughters rather than barter them
for sons, and some are sung from marine despair
by children's voices that they recognize
as home, *where all the waters meet.* The ballad

bears his burden, pours a corroded pail of gales
over his unwashed head to rust a trawler's net
of chain-mail armor in an undertow. The iron
found in the hand makes him a man

when Gower plays his red guitar.

II

Behold our hero, Pericles, once a man
of parts, and now a man apart
from banks and harbors, from anywhere
but wind-lashed waves and thunderheads. His plot
is wandering, the answer to his riddle

nowhere on earth. The hero is identified
by all the places left behind (*What seas, what shores,
what gray rocks and what islands*), his commerce
with the open sea, trading a wife
for an auspicious gale, a daughter for

safe landfall. Landless, a daughter trades
her talents for virginity, her qualities
for a customer become a husband
by a found father's will. Of her ledgers
of these transactions not a trace

remains, erased in recognition's tide
of tears: a current that will take her
back to a Tyre she's never seen, built on trade
in textiles, cinnabar, and wheat. So she has lost
a mother twice, and gained a governor for father

of her father's heirs, another woman traded
between two men of means to make the marriage plot.
And woodthrush calling through the fog, My
daughter. You'll wear purple, girl, and cloth-of-gold,
and spin your tale in tapestries no one will read.

Bring me spices, ink and paper, My casket
and my jewels. Bring me the satin coffin.

III

Thaisa loves a man of no renown, and with a name
to come. That's Homer, by way of Pound, and somewhat
misremembered. Like the play, like Pericles,

who misremembers who he is and has to be reminded
by a mislaid child, whom he has missed
without quite having met. (She is a woman

made of stone, a statue overlooking Tarsus
harbor, thighs sealed shut as a tomb, cold
to Lysimachus' advances. There is no private place, none

where they are not watched.) A text abducted
like a daughter pirates seize, the play predicts
its fragments, is predicated on them. A romance

that rounds upon itself (rousing but a bit
ridiculous, and recognizing itself so), this *song*
that old was sung revises its own tune. We may ascribe

the plot's lacunae to a nodding scribe, an actor's lapse
in memory, judgment. *Th'unfriendly elements*
forget thee utterly. We reconstruct the juncture

out of conjecture, and take our parts in the play:
the lines corrupt, and bracketed by gaps. Bracketed
by transactions in textiles and well-born virgins,

sea-tossed, Pericles thwarts one role after another, *driven
before the winds* over a painted backcloth wave,
scraps of wayward canvas sewn into a rotting sail. He's a prince

among men, this man she's set her course
on marrying before she knows his name: he never tires
of wandering from Tyre, *where we left him,*

on the sea. Knock on the moon and the stars
come out of clouds to guide his barque,
knock on the stars and the door is opened

to a temple in Ephesus where a coffined wife's cabochon
has navigated Neptune's sea of asterisks and breakers,
cast ashore like driftglass smoothed to opal, pearl:

the woman he weeps to lose and find alike.

DAVID CASE

Fear No More

Virginia Woolf has Mrs. Dalloway stop
outside the bookshop window, seeing
Cymbeline left open to Act IV,
Scene ii, reminding the dead
of their advantages:
"Fear no more the heat o' th' sun,
Nor the Furious winter's rages."
Does Clarissa believe it, even in London?
So much harder, then, in Pasadena
of Pet Metropolis, Cheesecake Factory,
the Huntington's Shakespeare Garden.
Still, I tell you, Cloten, *fear no more*
the mournful clouds of waste rose petals
kicked up the second of January.

ANNIE FINCH

Perdita's Song

We played by the water, ran barefoot,
opened our eyes and grew brown.
When did we stop and start growing
into the halls of tall stone?

Ophelia, Miranda, my sisters,
motherless daughters of men,
when were we told our inheritance
would be an untrodden silk hem?

Why did we turn from the water?
When did we find we had grown?
How did it turn out that water
was only a place we could drown?

KATHLEEN KIRK

Exit, Pursued by a Bear

This is Bohemia, lady.
Not a café or a lifestyle
but a land.
Oh, pardon me:
I see you know your way around.
I took you for an actress or an ingénue,
being elegant and thin,
soft-spoken and direct.
You did not start when I stepped out
from behind the tree,
and so I thought you an angel
or a fiction
or a paper cutout,
the caliber of Matisse.
I am an educated beast,
a virtual Caliban. Beware!
You do not even blink, though I know you see.
Where do you think you're going?
Wait for me.

CHARLES HARPER WEBB

At *The Tempest* with a Pregnant Wife

"The name *Caliban* derives from cannibal,"
The program states. A poor choice, then,
For a future M.D. Still, Cal Ripken
And his consecutive ball games, Cal Klein
And his jeans, Cal Worthy and his dog Spot
Could all be Calibans. The leap is shorter
Than *Archibald Leach* to *Cary Grant, Norma
Egstrom* to *Peggy Lee, Jack Rosenblum*
To *Werner Erhart.* My son "Cal" could
Grow up to be a movie star, a jazz singer,
A vacuum-cleaner-salesman-turned-guru
Who eats the flesh of his own kind.

Miranda is the modern felon's hacksaw-
In-the-birthday-cake. *Prospero*
Is the blue goop that gets toilets "cleaner
Than clean." The last *Ariel* played
Wicked Witch with herself in the oven.
But *Caliban* is virgin turf: a vacant lot
In a toney neighborhood, for sale cheap
Because some murders happened there.

I love how Caliban lumbers on stage,
Ragged as a molting fruit bat. I love
His curses, complaints, and thirst for revenge
On his master, who's the kind of control-
Geek who'll conjure you a kidney stone
Or a city inspector to count your cats
And make you raze your rumpus room.
Hell yes I feel like Caliban —
Overworked, underpaid, denied
The cover-girl daughter because I don't
Drive a Beemer, or have a best-seller,
And no one pays me to wear tennis shoes.

Caliban is elemental, same
As me — his mom, a hag; his dad, a devil
(Their detractors say). He loves the music
Wind makes twisting among trees. He loves
Cool water on his skin, and moderate sun.
He loves sweet berries, and red meat killed with his
Own hand. How can he be a cannibal?
In the whole world, there's no other of his kind.

STEPHEN COREY

The Tempest

to my daughter Miranda

If you name your daughter *vision*,
or *wondrous to behold*, you should not be surprised
if she comes to you in anger or in shame,
wishing to be known as *Mary* or *Ann*.
That will be the moment to carry her out
to the things of the world she is not,
speaking other sounds that were almost hers:
aspen, lily-white, cumulo-nimbus glow.

Soon enough she'll realize the world,
too often, gets named in hope of profit,
or deceit, or the scientist's exactitude.
But on the greening island of the family
testing its voice in the months of waiting,
the sought-after words are music and the past:
Grandparent. Aunt. Child deceased.

Spirits of fashion and monsters of commerce
lurk, bedfellows eager to keep us
from our own best inventions and songs.
Some days it seems we grow from wailing silence
into speech, only that we might curse
the coming return to silence.
But if you've named your daughter *wondrous to behold*,
she'll someday learn she heard those words
before all others, and then again, and again.
When you are gone beyond all roaring
she'll know, should you ever brave return,
which words are the first you'll speak.

MICHAEL B. STILLMAN

Prospero

You've been given keys
which would open
the great invisible halls of abstract hatred.

The very sunlight
exerts its own
will, controls you

living within the silences of this island, the green
and passionate stillness
reminding you

— will it last forever? —

at all hours, in all lights
of the persistence
of naked force,

that generous rape of the patient man's mind, that easelessness.

And yet, how steadfastly
something holds, you
refuse to open anything, refuse

to allow expression of absolute will its articulate entrance, not here.

Instead, the lyrical animals
move, and there are
sounds of occasional chimes.

How shall we understand
these gardens, this

woodpile, the stone depths
of the well

— that strenuous effort —

the honest mind, the refinement of your only daughter?
You have been given keys to abstract hatred, yet have stayed
outside, close
in touch with a various love of earth
for

the reception of its seasons, the mysteries of its changing weather.

J. P. DANCING BEAR

Caliban

Before hatred ate my heart
there was music:
my mother's willow music,
her dark willow music of wind and wave.
There was water singing over
the roots of ash, over stones.

Mother, I am a dead thing
with a voice trained for anything but song,

shackled in magic and pushed down,
taught to speak with a tongue
that damns with bellyaches.

Mother, your songs will die within me.
Mother, I am shaped an evil thing.
My tears run for the loss of song.
My fists clench for you.

J. P. DANCING BEAR

A Heart-Shaped Island

Prospero kept the island as his heart —
a secluded place far from the sight of ships
yet tensed, the open maw of a steel trap.
Scattered along the craggy shorelines
the planks of wrecked vessels drifted,
gray gulls cried like grieving sailors.
The underbrush rustled with dumb lust
as brutes smashed and searched in hunger.
At dusk gnats rose out of the reeds,
dark ghosts readying their haunts.
He left the night to the creatures
with their savage cacophony, each sure
it ruled the island, sure as his revenge.

KATHLEEN KIRK

Miranda

Much has been made of the island.
All my childhood is a sweet fantasy
of perfection,
though I was wild.
I took my father to be buried there
and it was hard to find.
No one has visited since,
but I do him honors of the mind,
a rather free-form rosemary
and an abstract rue.
He always liked these best.
The ills of government continue.
Oh, what a cure that would be!
Meantime I medicine myself,
as he taught me,
by falling into a trance of trust
and waking to detail,
a good life.
My grandchildren play
in a walled garden, away
from danger, there to watch
armies of red ants,
the bee with poison dart,
an occasional widow,
and the praying mantis —
a more than liberal education.
I know why we die.
'Tis from example.

EVA HOOKER
Ariel

Think on him: bound

to the inside of a tree, the inner bark

fast against his face and his lengthening

$\qquad\qquad\qquad\qquad$ limbs — his soft skull pinched

$\qquad$ by invisibility, or tied

$\qquad\qquad$ with cocooning

threads (made out of his own body) — the silk road of

the forest moth — with mouth

$\qquad\qquad$ groaning

as fast and loud, so loud *as mill-wheels strike*:

$\qquad$ like the moth eating his way out of quaint

$\qquad\qquad$ subjectivity, MAGICKED, and bent

to the springboard of nature

$\qquad\qquad$ cloven &
$\qquad\qquad$ correspondent to murmurings

$\qquad\qquad$ and vanishings and hunger

$\qquad\qquad\qquad\qquad$ which require shearing

of the surface

        bark of the brain

An emerald thing —

        :making is like that

        markings with black tree rings under the eye

        rise from the rift   and waft

        the Sea-wall

        cleaving the ribs, pegging

                and hooping   the Will

        :ear to the mouth, body stretched, feet upwards

Before the time be out

        (and thou must be subject)
        (to thyself)

Epilogue

STEPHEN COREY

Whatever Light

You dreamed the sound of your own name
was imbued with resonance,
could be offered to the world
just as you could stand at the curb
on a side street in Wichita
saying quietly, every few seconds,
"Shakespeare . . . Shakespeare . . . Shakespeare."
And you could leave knowing
you had touched some feeling
in nearly all who passed your slow chant:
The fat woman in the green dress
whose only boyfriend years before had tried
in earnest to recite the balcony scene.
The man who once walked howling from his broken home,
his dying daughter in his arms.

But you awoke to a name of no music or charm,
one that would roll from the bed
to stand alone waiting for first light
through the valanced brown curtains.
You knew that the glowing or dullness
in that day's particular light
would alter the tone of your voice.
You knew, whatever the light,
you would enter it that day
to speak to whatever ears
might still hear the music
you knew must exist.

Notes on Contributors

SYLVIA ADAMS is the author of the novel *This Weather of Hangmen* (1996) and of the poetry chapbook *Mondrian's Elephant*, which won the Cranberry Tree Press competition in 1998. She is teacher/facilitator for two Ottawa poetry groups and is on the board of *Alter Vox*, a Latin American periodical, which has translated some of her poems into Spanish.

Since 1977, GILBERT ALLEN has lived in Travelers Rest, South Carolina, with his wife, Barbara. He teaches at Furman University. His books are *In Everything* (1982), *Second Chances* (1991), *Commandments at Eleven* (1994), and *Driving to Distraction* (2003).

JAMES APPLEWHITE, born in a farming community in eastern North Carolina, has published nine books of poetry, his most recent being *Quartet for Three Voices* (2002). He teaches modern American poetry and writing at Duke University. He and his wife live in Durham on the edge of Eno River State Park.

RACHEL BECK lives in Iowa City, where she copyedits for the *Daily Iowan*. She is currently at work on her first book of poems and has been awarded a Michener-Engle fellowship. She has been a partisan of Emilia ever since watching the Guthrie Theater's 1993 production of *Othello*.

MARVIN BELL's latest books are *Nightworks: Poems 1962–2000* (2000) and *Rampant* (2004). For forty years he has taught for the Writers' Workshop at the University of Iowa.

JULIAN BERNICK, born in Fargo, North Dakota, attended Middlebury College and the Writers' Workshop at the University of Iowa and now lives in Minneapolis. His poems have appeared in *L'Ouverture*, *Curbside Review*, and *Poetry Motel*.

D. C. BERRY teaches at the Center for Writers at the University of Southern Mississippi in Hattiesburg. He recently won the *Black Warrior Review* chapbook contest with *Zen Cancer Saloon*, the account of his adventure with cancer of the spine.

DAVID CASE teaches English at Los Angeles City College and Pasadena City College. He is also an editor of *King Log* and pianist for the Amphion chamber group. His poetry has appeared in the *Southern Review*, *Carolina Quarterly*, and *Electronic Poetry Review*.

CHARLES CLIFTON teaches literature and creative writing at the Johnstown branch of the University of Pittsburgh. He writes poems and plays, looking for those stories that seem to be his in particular to tell.

NAN COHEN has published poems in *Poetry International*, *Prairie Schooner*, and *The Prentice-Hall Anthology of Women's Literature* (1999). She has held a Wallace Stegner

Fellowship and Jones Lectureship in Poetry at Stanford University and is a recipient of a 2003 NEA Fellowship.

JACK CONWAY'S newest book of poetry is *Life Sentences* (2002). His work has appeared in the *Antioch Review*, the *Columbia Review*, and *The Norton Book of Light Verse* (1986). He is an instructor at the Sarah Doyle Fiction Writers' Workshop at Brown University.

PETER COOLEY grew up in Detroit. He has published six books of poetry, the most recent being *A Place Made of Starlight* (2003). He was poetry editor for *North American Review* from 1970 to 2000, and since 1975 has taught creative writing at Tulane University in New Orleans.

The year 2003 marked the publication of STEPHEN COREY'S tenth poetry collection, *There Is No Finished World*, and his twentieth year on the editorial staff of the *Georgia Review*. He is currently completing a volume of essays, *She Is Startled at the Big Sound*, and working on another poetry collection, *The Complete Plays of William Shakespeare*.

ALFRED CORN lives in Rhode Island. He is the author of nine books of poetry, the most recent being *Contradictions* (2002). Among the awards he has received are a Guggenheim Fellowship, an NEA Fellowship, and a fellowship from the Academy of Arts and Letters. He has taught at Yale, Columbia, and Oklahoma State University.

SHERYL CORNETT teaches English and creative writing at North Carolina State University. Her work has been published in *Mars Hill Review, Image*, and the *Raleigh News and Observer*. She was a finalist for the 1999 Betts Fiction Prize established in honor of Doris Betts.

KATHERINE COTTLE holds an MFA in creative writing from the University of Maryland at College Park. Her work has appeared in *Willow Springs, Puerto del Sol*, and the *Greensboro Review*. She lives in Glen Arm, Maryland, with her husband and son.

PETER CUMMINGS teaches English and comparative literature, primarily Shakespeare, at Hobart and William Smith Colleges in Geneva, New York. Apart from literature he is passionate about long-distance cycling, kayaking, and violin- and viola-making. He admits an addiction to the sonnet form and has written more than five hundred of them.

J. P. DANCING BEAR'S poems have appeared in *Atlanta Review, Seattle Review*, and *Permafrost*. He is editor in chief of the *American Poetry Journal* and the host of *Out of Our Minds*, a weekly poetry program on public radio station KKUP in Santa Clara, California. He is the winner of the 2002 Slipstream Press Poetry Prize for his chapbook *What Language*; his full-length collection is *Billy Last Crow* (2004).

CHAD DAVIDSON'S recent collection, *Consolation Miracle* (2003), was winner of the Crab Orchard Prize. He is an assistant professor of English at the University of West Georgia.

KIRSTEN DIERKING lives in Arden Hills, Minnesota. She is the author of the poetry collection *One Red Eye* (2001) and the winner of a poetry fellowship from the Minnesota State Arts Board and a Career Initiative grant from the Loft Literary Center. She received her master's degree in creative writing from Hamline University.

ELON G. EIDENIER is Bookman in Charge of the Gothic Bookshop at Duke University. He has published a book of poetry titled *Sonnets to Eurydice* (1976), and his poems have appeared in numerous journals, including the *Virginia Quarterly Review*, *Ruah*, and *Rhino*. He lives with his wife, Betty, in Hillsborough, North Carolina.

SANDY FEINSTEIN is an associate professor of English and honors coordinator at the Penn State Berks-Lehigh Valley College. She has published poetry in *Facture* and *Fait Accomplit*. She also publishes scholarly work on the Middle Ages and Renaissance, including a recent article titled "Crossbows, Lutes, and Coitus" in *Exemplaria*.

ANNIE FINCH'S books of poetry include *Eve* (1997), *Calendars* (2003), and a reissue of her 1982 long poem *The Encyclopedia of Scotland* (forthcoming). Her translations include the *Complete Poems of Louise Labé*, and her collection of essays *The Heart of Poetry* is forthcoming.

ALICE FRIMAN'S latest book, *Zoo* (1999), won the Ezra Pound Poetry Award from Truman State University and the Sheila Motton Prize from the New England Poetry Club. She has received fellowships from the Indiana Arts Commission, the Arts Council of Indianapolis, and the Bernheim Foundation. In 2001 she won the James Boatwright Prize from *Shenandoah*. She now makes her home in Georgia.

CARMEN GERMAIN teaches at Peninsula College in Port Angeles, Washington, where she is codirector of the Foothills Writers Series. She has written a chapbook, *Living Room, Earth* (2002).

WILLIAM GREENWAY'S seventh collection of poems, *Ascending Order*, was published in 2003. He coedited the collection *I Have My Own Song for It: Modern Poems of Ohio* (2002). He is the recipient of the 2001 Ohioana Poetry Award and is a professor of English at Youngstown State University.

KEVIN GRIFFITH is an associate professor of English at Capital University in Columbus, Ohio. He has received two Individual Artist Fellowships in poetry from the Ohio Arts Council. His latest book of poems is *Paradise Refunded* (1999).

R. S. GWYNN'S most recent collection is *No Word of Farewell: Selected Poems 1970–2000* (2001). He is the editor of the Pocket Anthology series from Penguin Academics and is a frequent contributor of book reviews to the *Hudson Review* and the *Sewanee Review*. He is University Professor of English at Lamar University in Beaumont, Texas.

H. PALMER HALL'S most recent collection is *Reflections on Publishing, Writing and Other Things* (2003). His work has appeared in the *North American Review*, the *Texas*

Review, and *Ascent*. He is the library director at St. Mary's University in San Antonio, where he also directs Pecan Grove Press.

LEILANI HALL is an assistant professor of English at California State University, Northridge, where she teaches creative writing and theory. She received second place in the 2003 Jane Kenyon Poetry Prize and has published in the *Laurel Review*, the *Journal*, and the *North American Review*.

RICHARD HEDDERMAN lives in York Harbor, Maine. His poems have appeared in *South Dakota Review*, *Cutbank*, and *Puckerbrush*, and his cycle based on *Beowulf* was recently published in the Welsh language literary journal *Skald*. He is an active theater professional specializing in stage combat.

EVA HOOKER teaches Shakespeare and creative writing at Saint John's University, Collegeville, Minnesota. *The Winter Keeper*, a hand-sewn chapbook, was a finalist for the Minnesota Book Award in poetry in 2001. Her poems have appeared in *Harvard Review*, *Salmagundi*, and *Orion*. She is a member of the religious order Sisters of the Holy Cross.

DAN JOHNSON's books of poetry are *Suggestions from the Border* (1983), *Glance West* (1989), and *Come Looking* (1995). His poems have appeared in *West Branch*, *Rattle*, and *Southern Poetry Review*. He lives in Arlington, Virginia, and is a speechwriter for the director of the National Science Foundation.

ALLISON JOSEPH lives, writes, and teaches in Carbondale, Illinois, where she is on the faculty of Southern Illinois University. She also serves as editor of *Crab Orchard Review* and director of the Young Writers Workshop, a summer conference for high school creative writers. Her books of poems include *In Every Seam* (1997), *Imitation of Life* (1997), and *Worldly Pleasures* (2004).

KIRSTEN KASCHOCK is the author of the poetry collection *Unfathoms* (2003). She earned an MFA in poetry from Syracuse University and an MFA in dance from the University of Iowa. She is currently a PhD student at the University of Georgia.

J. KATES is a poet and literary translator who lives in Fitzwilliam, New Hampshire.

JENNIFER HILL KAUCHER's first book of poetry is *Questioning Walls Open* (2001). She owns and operates Wordpainting, a design and publishing studio in Edwardsville, Pennsylvania, and conducts poetry residencies and workshops throughout the state.

MELANIE KENNY received her MFA in poetry from Washington University in St. Louis, where she now lives. She is a native of Michigan's Upper Peninsula and grew up on the shores of Lake Superior. As an undergraduate at the University of Michigan, she received two Hopwood Awards in Poetry.

KATHLEEN KIRK lives in Normal, Illinois. She is a coeditor of *RHINO Magazine* and the editor of *Where We Live: Illinois Poets*, an anthology that emerged from a reading series supported by the American Library Association and the Illinois Arts Council. Her work has appeared in *Callaloo*, *Willow Review*, and *Quarter after Eight*.

RON KOERTGE'S latest book of poems is *Geography of the Forehead* (2000). He is also the author of fiction for young adults, including *Stoner & Spaz* (2002). He claims to be a fair to middling handicapper of thoroughbred racehorses.

MICHELLE LABARRE teaches in the equestrian program and the writing department of Houghton College in western New York. She lives with and responds to *retinitis pigmentosa*, a degenerative disease that typically expresses itself in night blindness and tunnel vision and that may advance to total blindness.

DANUSHA LAMÉRIS DE GARZA lives in Santa Cruz, California. She has published poems in *El Andar*, *Crab Orchard Review*, and *Water-Stone*, and is currently at work on her first collection.

ANN LAUINGER lives in Ossining, New York. Her book *Persuasions of the Fall* (2004) was winner of the first Agha Shahid Ali Prize in Poetry. She is a member of the literature faculty at Sarah Lawrence College.

By day, DEBORAH LEITER is an information architect, organizing content for the websites of Zondervan, a division of HarperCollins. On her nights and weekends, she is the book review editor for NightsAndWeekends.com, as well as the web editor for WorkingPOET, an online advice journal for poets. She lives in Grand Rapids, Michigan.

DIANE LOCKWARD'S first full-length book is *Eve's Red Dress* (2003). Her work has been featured on *Poetry Daily*, read by Garrison Keillor on *The Writer's Almanac*, and nominated for three Pushcart Prizes. She is the recipient of a 2003 fellowship from the New Jersey State Council on the Arts.

A former classics professor, ANTHONY LOMBARDY is working currently on a narrative poem about the recent history of the Sudan. His poems have appeared in the *National Review*, the *Hudson Review*, and the *New Yorker*. His collections of poetry include *Antique Collecting* (2004) and *Severe* (with Barbara Wallace, 1995).

KATHLEEN LYNCH is the author of *Greatest Hits* (2002), *No Spring Chicken* (2001), *Alterations of Rising* (2001), and *How to Build an Owl* (1995). A poet, fiction writer, and artist, she lives in Carmichael, California.

MARJORIE MADDOX is a professor of English at Lock Haven University in Pennsylvania. She has published *Perpendicular as I* (2003), *When the Wood Clacks Out Your Name* (2002), *Body Parts* (1999), *Ecclesia* (1997), *How to Fit God into a Poem* (1993), and *Nightrider to Edinburgh* (1986).

MARY MAKOFSKE is an assistant professor of English at Orange County Community College in New York. She is the author of *Eating Nasturtiums* (1998) and *The Disappearance of Gargoyles* (1988). She is also the recipient of the Robert Penn Warren Poetry Prize, the *Lullwater Review* Poetry Prize, and the *Spoon River Review* Poetry Prize. Her poems have appeared in *Poetry*, *Mississippi Review*, and the *North American Review*.

ADRIANNE MARCUS lives in San Rafael, California, with her husband, the futurist Ian H. Wilson. In addition to poetry, she writes stories, novels, and nonfiction.

She publishes in *Paris Review, Cosmopolitan, Food & Wine, Town & Country, Travel & Leisure,* and in her words, "anything else with an ampersand in it."

STEVEN MARX teaches English at California Polytechnic State University in San Luis Obispo. He is the author of *Shakespeare and the Bible* (2000).

LEE MCCARTHY lives in Bakersfield, California. Her poetry collections include *Desire's Door* (1991), *Combing Hair with a Seashell* (1992), and *Good Girl* (2002). Valley Public Radio has featured some of her short fiction in recent years.

PETER MEINKE has published twelve books of poetry, the most recent being *Zinc Fingers* (2000). His story collection, *The Piano Tuner*, received the 1986 Flannery O'Connor Award. He has recently been appointed to the Darden Endowed Chair in Creative Writing at Old Dominion University in Norfolk, Virginia.

JUDITH H. MONTGOMERY lives in Bend, Oregon. Her poems have appeared in *Bellingham Review*, the *Southern Review*, and *Gulf Coast*. Her chapbook, *Passion*, received the 2000 Oregon Book Award for Poetry. Her work has been nominated for a Pushcart Prize and has received the National Writers' Union, *Red Rock*, and *Americas Review* poetry prizes.

JANICE TOWNLEY MOORE is chair of the humanities division at Young Harris College in Georgia. She has published recent poetry in the *Georgia Review* and *Prairie Schooner*.

HARRYETTE MULLEN was born in Florence, Alabama, and raised in Fort Worth, Texas. Her books of poetry include *Sleeping with the Dictionary* (2002) and *Muse and Drudge* (1995). She teaches African American literature and creative writing at the University of California, Los Angeles.

J. B. MULLIGAN lives in Washingtonville, New York. His poems and stories have appeared in *Rearview Quarterly*, the *Comstock Review*, and *Numbat*.

LEONARD NATHAN has published over a dozen volumes of poetry, the latest being *Tears of the Old Magician* (2003). He is also the author of a prose book, *Diary of a Left-Handed Birdwatcher* (1996). He is retired from the University of California, Berkeley, and lives with his wife in Kensington, California.

DAVID OLIVEIRA is the author of *In the Presence of Snakes* (2000) and a collaborator in *A Near Country: Poems of Loss* (1999). His poems are anthologized in *California Poetry from the Gold Rush to the Present* (2004); *The Geography of Home: California's Poetry of Place* (1999); and *How Much Earth: The Fresno Poets* (2001), which he coedited with Christopher Buckley and M. L. Williams. He is the first poet laureate of Santa Barbara, California, and lives in Phnom Penh, Cambodia.

LEE PATTON writes poetry, fiction, and drama in Denver. His poems have appeared in the *Threepenny Review*, the *Massachusetts Review*, and *California Quarterly*. His novel *Nothing Gold Can Stay* was a finalist for the 2001 Lambda Award, and his drama has been awarded the Borderlands Playwrights Prize (*The Houseguest*) and the Ashland New Playwrights Prize (*Orwell in Orlando*).

JIM PETERSON's most recent collection is *The Owning Stone* (2000), winner of the Benjamin Saltman Award. Also forthcoming are a novel, *Paper Crown*, and another poetry collection, *The Last Child*. His poetry was awarded a 2002–2003 fellowship from the Virginia Arts Council. He is currently the coordinator of creative writing at Randolph-Macon Woman's College in Lynchburg, Virginia.

KEN POBO's newest book of poems is *Introductions* (2003). His chapbook *Greatest Hits* came out in 2002. He teaches literature and creative writing at Widener University in Pennsylvania.

ARTHUR POWERS lives in Brazil, where he has done volunteer work with the Peace Corps and the Franciscans. His poems have appeared in *Americas Review*, the *Kansas Quarterly*, and the *Southern Poetry Review*, and he serves as a guest editor for *New Song*. His fiction has been recognized by the Massachusetts Artists Foundation and the National Catholic Press Association.

JOAN RAYMUND grew up in Los Angeles and is now retired in Ojai, California. She has just published the fifteenth edition of *Rivertalk*, an anthology of Ojai Valley poetry.

ZACK ROGOW's fifth book of poems is *Greatest Hits: 1979–2001*. He is an award-winning translator of French literature and editor of a new anthology of United States poetry, *The Face of Poetry* (2003). At the University of California, Berkeley, he coordinates the Lunch Poems Reading Series. He teaches in the MFA in Writing Program at the California College of the Arts in Oakland.

EDWIN ROMOND was a high school English teacher for thirty-two years. He is the author of *Blue Mountain Time: New and Selected Poems about Baseball* (2002), *Macaroons* (1997), and *Home Fire* (1993). He lives in Wind Gap, Pennsylvania, with his wife, Mary, and their son, Liam.

Raised in Southern California, TANIA RUNYAN received her MFA from Bowling Green State University and now lives in Mundelein, Illinois. Her work has appeared in *Poetry*, *Southern Poetry Review*, and *Poetry Northwest*. She is currently at work on a collection of poems about martyrs.

SHEROD SANTOS's most recent collection is *The Perishing* (2003). His previous collection, *The Pilot Star Elegies* (2002), received the Theodore Roethke Memorial Award and was a National Book Award Finalist. His book of literary essays, *A Poetry of Two Minds* (2000), was a finalist for the National Book Critics Circle Award in Criticism. He is the Curators' Distinguished Professor of Literature at the University of Missouri-Columbia, where he is the director of the Center for the Literary Arts.

REGINALD SHEPHERD lives and writes in Pensacola, Florida. His four books of poems are *Otherhood* (2003); *Wrong* (1999); *Angel, Interrupted* (1996); and *Some Are Drowning* (1994). Winner of a 1993 Nation/"Discovery" Award, he has received grants from the NEA, the Illinois Arts Council, and the Constance Saltonstall Foundation. His work has appeared in four editions of *The Best American Poetry*.

MAURYA SIMON is the recipient of a 1999–2000 NEA Fellowship in poetry, as well as the author of six volumes of poetry, most recently *Ghost Orchid* (2004) and *A Brief History of Punctuation* (2002). She teaches poetry at the University of California, Riverside, and lives in the Angeles National Forest.

FLOYD SKLOOT's poems have appeared in the *Atlantic*, *Harper's*, and the *Hudson Review*. He has published three collections, including *The Evening Light*, which won the 2001 Oregon Book Award in Poetry. His fourth collection, *The End of Dreams*, will appear in spring 2005. He has also published three novels, a memoir of the illness experience, and a collection of essays.

ELLEN MCGRATH SMITH is a visiting lecturer in literature and writing at the University of Pittsburgh, where she received an MFA in poetry in 1993. Her work has appeared in *Southern Poetry Review*, *Artful Dodge*, and *Denver Quarterly*. Her chapbook, *The Dog Makes Its Rounds and Other Poems*, was published in 2002. She is the recipient of an Academy of American Poets Prize.

J. D. SMITH lives in Washington, D. C. Recent publications include the edited anthology *Northern Music: Poems about and Inspired by Glenn Gould* (2001) and *The Hypothetical Landscape* (1999). His writing in several genres has appeared in *Chelsea*, *Connecticut Review*, and *Pleiades*.

BARRY SPACKS is a writing and literature professor at the University of California, Santa Barbara, after many years of teaching at the Massachusetts Institute of Technology. He has published two novels and nine poetry collections, the most recent of which are *The Hope of the Air* (2004) and *Regarding Women* (2004), winner of the Cherry Grove Prize.

WILLIAM STAFFORD (1914–1993) won the National Book Award for *Traveling Through the Dark* (1962). Born in Kansas, he taught for many years at Lewis and Clark College in Oregon and died a beloved man. His posthumous collection of new and selected poems is *The Way It Is* (1998).

BRIAN STAVELEY did his undergraduate work at Dartmouth College, where he was awarded the Grimes Prize for the best manuscript of original poetry. While pursuing a master's degree in creative writing at Boston University, he was awarded the Academy of American Poets Prize as well as the Robert Fitzgerald Prize for literary translation. His work appears in *Literary Imagination* and the *Larcom Review*, and he currently reads for *Agni*.

Originally from the coast of Virginia, MICHAEL B. STILLMAN migrated to California in 1968, bringing with him a passion for Renaissance drama. "Songs for the Seasons" was written in response to a performance of *Love's Labor's Lost* directed by Daniel Seltzer at the Loeb Drama Center. He is a musician as well as a poet and lives in Palo Alto.

LEON STOKESBURY's most recent book, *Autumn Rhythm: New and Selected Poems*, was awarded the Poets Prize in 1998. He teaches poetry and creative writing at Georgia State University in Atlanta.

KATHERINE SWIGGART is a graduate of the Writers' Workshop at the University of Iowa and has published poems in *Columbia, Helicon Anthological Journal of Contemporary Poetry*, and *Writers at Work*. She is coeditor of the *Electronic Poetry Review* and teaches at Willamette University in Salem, Oregon.

CHRIS TERRIO lives in New York City. He recently finished a screen adaptation of Barry Werth's biography *The Scarlet Professor*, based on the life of the literary critic Newton Arvin, and directed an original screenplay for Merchant Ivory Productions in 2004. He is working on a book of poetry.

SUSAN TERRIS'S most recent books of poetry are *Fire Is Favorable to the Dreamer* (2003), *Eye of the Holocaust* (1999), and *Curved Space* (1998). Forthcoming collections are *Poetic License* and *Natural Defenses*. Her young adult fiction includes *Nell's Quilt* (1987). With C. B. Follett, she is coeditor of an annual anthology, *Runes: A Review of Poetry*.

LEE UPTON'S fourth book of poetry is *Civilian Histories* (2000), and her third book of literary criticism is *The Muse of Abandonment* (1998). She is a professor of English and writer-in-residence at Lafayette College in Easton, Pennsylvania.

RYAN G. VAN CLEAVE lives in South Carolina. His most recent books include a poetry collection, *The Magical Breasts of Britney Spears* (2004), and a creative writing textbook, *Contemporary American Poetry: Behind the Scenes* (2003). He teaches at Clemson University.

JEANNE MURRAY WALKER'S most recent book of poetry is *A Deed to the Light* (2004). Her poems have appeared in *Poetry, Image*, and the *Georgia Review*. Among her awards are an NEA Fellowship and a Pew Fellowship in the Arts. She is on the editorial board of *Shenandoah*, and her work has appeared with Poetry in Motion on busses and trains.

BJ WARD'S third book of poetry, *Gravedigger's Birthday* (2002), was a finalist for the Paterson Poetry Prize. He is the recipient of a 2004 Pushcart Prize for poetry and a 2003 Distinguished Artist Poetry Fellowship from the New Jersey State Council on the Arts. His work has been featured on National Public Radio and *Poetry Daily*, and published in *Tri-Quarterly, Poetry*, and *Natural Bridge*.

WILLIAM JOHN WATKINS is a member of the founding faculty at Brookdale Community College in Lincroft, New Jersey, where he teaches early American literature. His poems have appeared in the *South Carolina Review, Nimrod*, and *Commonweal*. His sonnet "Wife of My Youth, Look Back, Look Back" won the 1994 *Hellas* Award.

CHARLES HARPER WEBB'S most recent collection is *Tulip Farms and Leper Colonies* (2001). He is editor of *Stand Up Poetry: An Expanded Anthology* (U of Iowa P, 2002). The recipient of grants from the Whiting and Guggenheim foundations, he teaches at California State University, Long Beach.

JACKSON WHEELER, a native of the mountains of North Carolina, now lives in Oxnard, California, where he coordinates a poetry series at the Carnegie Art

Museum. A social worker, he is the author of *Swimming Past Iceland* (1993) and coauthor of *A Near Country: Poems of Loss* (1999).

GAIL WHITE lives in Breaux Bridge, Louisiana, on the banks of Bayou Teche. Her latest book is *The Price of Everything* (2002). She also coedited the anthology *The Muse Strikes Back* (1997) and is working on a new book of short verse.

DANIEL WILLIAMS has been a resident of and poet to the Sierra Nevada region of northern California for thirty years. He currently lives and works in Yosemite National Park.

CECILIA WOLOCH is the director of Summer Poetry in Idyllwild, California, and serves on the faculty of the MFA Program in Poetry at New England College. Her books of poetry are *Late* (2003), *Tsigan: The Gypsy Poem* (2002), and *Sacrifice* (1997). She maintains residences in both Atlanta and Los Angeles.

DAVID WRIGHT teaches writing and literature at Wheaton College in Illinois. His most recent collection is *A Liturgy for Stones* (2003). His poems and essays have appeared in *Christian Century*, *Midwest Quarterly*, and the *Mennonite Quarterly Review*.

TRACY S. YOUNGBLOM holds an MA from the University of St. Thomas in St. Paul, Minnesota, and an MFA from Warren Wilson College in Asheville, North Carolina. Her poems have appeared in *Shenandoah*, *Slate*, and *Great River Review*. She teaches writing at the college level and lives in Minneapolis with her family, including three sons and a female dog that, she says, exists in a state of fine frenzy.

Acknowledgments

All epigraph quotations from Shakespeare are taken from *The Riverside Shakespeare*, 2nd ed., ed. G. Blakemore Evans et al. (Boston: Houghton, 1997). Quotations within the poems themselves derive from various editions.

Grateful acknowledgment is made to the poets and to the editors of the publications in which some of the poems in this anthology first appeared.

Sylvia Adams: "Shakespeare's Eyebrows" appeared in *Vintage '97–'98* (Quarry Press, 1998). Reprinted by permission of the poet.

Gilbert Allen: "The Good Duke Speaks" appeared in *In Everything*, by Gilbert Allen (Lotus, 1982). Reprinted by permission of the poet.

James Applewhite: "On the Mississippi" appeared in *Mississippi Review*. Reprinted by permission of the poet.

Rachel Beck: "Epilogue for Emilia" is printed by permission of the poet.

Rachel Beck: "Interlude" is printed by permission of the poet.

Marvin Bell: "Shakespeare's Wages" appeared in *Shakespeare's Wages*, by Marvin Bell (Carlsen Fine Print Editions, 2004). Reprinted by permission of the poet.

Marvin Bell: "Sounds of the Resurrected Dead Man's Footsteps (#1)" appeared in *Nightworks: Poems 1962–2000*, by Marvin Bell (Copper Canyon Press, 2000). Reprinted by permission of the poet and of Copper Canyon Press.

Julian Bernick: "Iago" is printed by permission of the poet.

D. C. Berry: "Hambone Two Tongue" appeared in *Adirondack Review*. Reprinted by permission of the poet.

David Case: "Fear No More" is printed by permission of the poet.

Charles Clifton: "Lear Drives His Rambler across Laurel Mountain" is printed by permission of the poet.

Nan Cohen: "Horatio" appeared in *Cider Press Review*. Reprinted by permission of the poet.

Jack Conway: "This Is What Happens When You Let Hamlet Play Quarterback" is printed by permission of the poet.

Peter Cooley: "For Hamlet" appeared in *Sacred Conversations*, by Peter Cooley (Carnegie Mellon, 1998) and in *Mississippi Review*. Reprinted by permission of the poet.

Stephen Corey: "The Tempest" appeared in *All These Lands You Call One Country*, by Stephen Corey (University of Missouri Press, 1992). Reprinted by permission of the poet.

Stephen Corey: "Understanding *King Lear*" appeared in *Synchronized Swimming*, by Stephen Corey (Swallow's Tale Press, 1985; Livingston Press, 1993). Reprinted by permission of the poet.

Stephen Corey: "Whatever Light" appeared in *Synchronized Swimming*, by Stephen Corey (Swallow's Tale Press, 1985; Livingston Press, 1993). Reprinted by permission of the poet.

Alfred Corn: "Reading *Pericles* in New London" appeared in *The Various Light*, by Alfred Corn (Viking Penguin, 1980). Reprinted by permission of the poet.

Sheryl Cornett: "Lear Expands His Last Words to Cordelia" is printed by permission of the poet.

Katherine Cottle: "My Poetess' Eyes" is printed by permission of the poet.

Peter Cummings: "Hamlet to Ophelia" appeared in *Mississippi Review*. Reprinted by permission of the poet.

J. P. Dancing Bear: "Caliban" appeared in *Zuzu's Petals Quarterly*. Reprinted by permission of the poet.

J. P. Dancing Bear: "Heart-Shaped Island" appeared in *Valparaiso Poetry Review*. Reprinted by permission of the poet.

J. P. Dancing Bear: "Iago, the Poet" is printed by permission of the poet.

Chad Davidson: "I Took by the Throat the Circumcised Dog" is printed by permission of the poet.

Kirsten Dierking: "Delacroix's Version" appeared in *One Red Eye*, by Kirsten Dierking (Holy Cow! Press, 2001). Reprinted by permission of the poet.

Elon G. Eidenier: "The Failure of Language" is printed by permission of the poet.

Sandy Feinstein: "The Catch" is printed by permission of the poet.

Sandy Feinstein: "Tendered" is printed by permission of the poet.

Annie Finch: "Perdita's Song" is printed by permission of the poet.

Alice Friman: "Diapers for My Father" appeared in the *Ohio Review* and in *Zoo*, by Alice Friman (University of Arkansas Press, 1999). Reprinted by permission of the poet.

Alice Friman: "Ophelia" appeared in the *Laurel Review* and in *Inverted Fire*, by Alice Friman (BkMk Press, 1997). Reprinted by permission of the poet.

Carmen Germain: "Literature 100" appeared in *Hurricane Alice*. Reprinted by permission of the poet.

William Greenway: "Ophelia Writes Home" appeared in *Mississippi Review*. Reprinted by permission of the poet.

Kevin Griffith: "Hamlet Meets Frankenstein" appeared in *Salt Hill Journal* and *Mississippi Review*. Reprinted by permission of the poet.

R. S. Gwynn: "Horatio's Philosophy" appeared in *No Word of Farewell: Selected Poems 1970–2000*, by R. S. Gwynn (Story Line Press, 2001). Reprinted by permission of the poet.

R. S. Gwynn: "Iago to His Torturers" appeared in *The Drive-In*, by R. S. Gwynn (University of Missouri Press, 1986) and in *No Word of Farewell: Selected Poems 1970–2000*, by R. S. Gwynn (Story Line Press, 2001). Reprinted by permission of the poet.

R. S. Gwynn: "Shakespearean Sonnet" is printed by permission of the poet.

H. Palmer Hall: "Romeo Is Dead" is printed by permission of the poet.

Leilani Hall: "Ophelia's Rant before She's Heavy with Drink" appeared in *Mississippi Review*. Reprinted by permission of the poet.

Richard Hedderman: "The First Player's Monologue" is printed by permission of the poet.

Richard Hedderman: "Ophelia" appeared in *Negative Capability*. Reprinted by permission of the poet.

Eva Hooker: "Ariel" appeared in *Salmagundi*. Reprinted by permission of the poet.

Eva Hooker: "What Bottom Said When He Came Home" appeared in *The Winter Keeper*, by Eva Hooker (Chapiteau Press, 2000). Reprinted by permission of the poet.

Dan Johnson: "Maybe Desdemona" appeared in *Come Looking*, by Dan Johnson (Washington Writers' Publishing House, 1985). Reprinted by permission of the poet.

Allison Joseph: "Not Ophelia" appeared in the *Mochila Review*. Reprinted by permission of the poet.

Kirsten Kaschock: "As Birds in Rain" appeared in *Unfathoms*, by Kirsten Kaschock (Slope Editions, 2003). Reprinted by permission of the poet.

J. Kates: "Nothing in Art" appeared in the *Chowder Review*. Reprinted by permission of the poet.

Jennifer Hill Kaucher: "Reading *Othello* and Watching a Girl Skip Rope" is printed by permission of the poet.

Melanie Kenny: "Hungry as the Sea" appeared in the *Beloit Journal*. Reprinted by permission of the poet.

Kathleen Kirk: "Exit, Pursued by a Bear" is printed by permission of the poet.

Kathleen Kirk: "Lavinia" is printed by permission of the poet.

Kathleen Kirk: "Miranda" is printed by permission of the poet.

Kathleen Kirk: "Portia" is printed by permission of the poet.

Ron Koertge: "My Students" is printed by permission of the poet.

Michelle LaBarre: "For Gloucester on Being Newly Blind" appeared in *The Lanthorn*. Reprinted by permission of the poet.

Danusha Laméris de Garza: "Act One" is printed by permission of the poet.

Ann Lauinger: "Three Songs for *King Leir*" appeared in *Persuasions of Fall*, by Ann Lauinger (University of Utah Press, 2004). Reprinted by permission of the poet and of the University of Utah Press.

Deborah Leiter: "Midsummer's Eve" is printed by permission of the poet.

Diane Lockward: "On First Reading *Romeo and Juliet*" appeared in *Eve's Red Dress*, by Diane Lockward (Wind Publications, 2003). Reprinted by permission of the poet.

Anthony Lombardy: "Shall I Compare Thee . . . ?" appeared in *Antique Collecting*, by Anthony Lombardy (WordTech Editions, 2004). Reprinted by permission of the poet.

Kathleen Lynch: "Ophelia in Utah" is printed by permission of the poet.

Marjorie Maddox: "Cancer Diagnosis" is printed by permission of the poet.

Mary Makofske: "Viola, to Olivia" appeared in *Calyx* and in *The Disappearance of Gargoyles*, by Mary Makofske (Thorntree Press, 1988). Reprinted by permission of the poet.

Adrianne Marcus: "Cleopatra" appeared in *Woman Poet* and in *Child of Earthquake Country*, by Adrianne Marcus (New World Press, 1980). Reprinted by permission of the poet.

Steven Marx: "Mark Antony's Valentine" is printed by permission of the poet.

Lee McCarthy: "Running Loose around the Castle" appeared in *Rivertalk* and in *Good Girl*, by Lee McCarthy (Story Line Press, 2002). Reprinted by permission of the poet and of Story Line Press.

Peter Meinke: "Blow, Blow, Thou Winter Wind" appeared in *Scars*, by Peter Meinke (University of Pittsburgh Press, 1996). Reprinted by permission of the poet and of the University of Pittsburgh Press.

Peter Meinke: "Noreen" appeared in *Scars*, by Peter Meinke (University of Pittsburgh Press, 1996). Reprinted by permission of the poet and of the University of Pittsburgh Press.

Judith H. Montgomery: "Ophelia, in Winter" appeared in *Gulf Coast*. Reprinted by permission of the poet.

Janice Townley Moore: "To Love That Well" appeared in *Southern Humanities Review*. Reprinted by permission of the poet and of *Southern Humanities Review*.

Harryette Mullen: "Dim Lady" appeared in *Sleeping with the Dictionary*, by Harryette Mullen (University of California Press, 2002). Reprinted by permission of the poet.

J. B. Mulligan: "Shylock" is printed by permission of the poet.

Leonard Nathan: "Making a Love Poem" appeared in *Tears of the Old Magician*, by Leonard Nathan (Orchises Press, 2003). Reprinted by permission of the poet.

Leonard Nathan: "Ragged Sonnet: So Shall I Live" appeared in *Salmagundi*. Reprinted by permission of the poet.

Leonard Nathan: "Ragged Sonnet: When in a Deep Depression" appeared in *Edge City Review*. Reprinted by permission of the poet.

David Oliveira: "Laurence Olivier's Hamlet" is printed by permission of the poet.

Lee Patton: "When Everything Is Goneril" appeared in the *Threepenny Review*. Reprinted by permission of the poet.

Jim Peterson: "As If" is printed by permission of the poet.

Ken Pobo: "Stormy Lear" is printed by permission of the poet.

Arthur Powers: "Iago" is printed by permission of the poet.

Joan Raymund: "The Ordeal of Love" is printed by permission of the poet.

Zack Rogow: "Symmetron: You and Brother Will" is printed by permission of the poet.

Edwin Romond: "Lady Macbeth, Afterward" is printed by permission of the poet.

Tania Runyan: "Teaching Shakespeare" is printed by permission of the poet.

Sherod Santos: "Romeo & Juliet" appeared in *Slate* and in *The Perishing*, by Sherod Santos (Norton, 2003). Reprinted by permission of the poet and of W. W. Norton.

Reginald Shepherd: "*Pericles: Prince of Tyre*: A Commentary" appeared in *Angel, Interrupted*, by Reginald Shepherd (University of Pittsburgh Press, 1996). Reprinted by permission of the poet and of the University of Pittsburgh Press.

Reginald Shepherd: "Snowdrops and Summer Snowflakes, Drooping" appeared in *TriQuarterly*. Reprinted by permission of the poet.

Maurya Simon: "Helsinore, Denmark" appeared in *Mississippi Review*. Reprinted by permission of the poet.

Floyd Skloot: "The Role of a Lifetime" appeared in *Virginia Quarterly Review*. Reprinted by permission of the poet.

Ellen McGrath Smith: Selections from "Shaken" are printed by permission of the poet.

J. D. Smith: "Goodsonnet" is printed by permission of the poet.

J. D. Smith: "Seven Ages of Man" appeared in *Light*. Reprinted by permission of the poet.

Barry Spacks: "The Film Version" is printed by permission of the poet.

William Stafford: "Owls at the Shakespeare Festival" appeared in *An Oregon Message*, by William Stafford (Harper and Row, 1987). Reprinted by permission of the Estate of William Stafford.

Brian Stavely: "Speak Again" is printed by permission of the poet.

Michael B. Stillman: "Ophelia" appeared in *Sequoia*. Reprinted by permission of the poet.

Michael B. Stillman: "Prospero" appeared in *Sequoia*. Reprinted by permission of the poet.

Michael B. Stillman: "Songs for the Seasons: A Distant Collaboration" appeared in *Sequoia*. Reprinted by permission of the poet.

Michael B. Stillman: "The Two Princes" appeared in *Sequoia*. Reprinted by permission of the poet.

Leon Stokesbury: "Bottom's Dream" appeared in *Autumn Rhythm: New and Selected Poems*, by Leon Stokesbury (University of Arkansas Press, 1998). Reprinted by permission of the poet.

Leon Stokesbury: "Jaques Lured by Audrey" appeared in *Autumn Rhythm: New and Selected Poems*, by Leon Stokesbury (University of Arkansas Press, 1998). Reprinted by permission of the poet.

Leon Stokesbury: "Reynaldo in Paris" appeared in *Autumn Rhythm: New and Selected Poems*, by Leon Stokesbury (University of Arkansas Press, 1998). Reprinted by permission of the poet.

Katherine Swiggart: "The Exhaled" is printed by permission of the poet.

Chris Terrio: "Viola Recalls" is printed by permission of the poet.

Susan Terris: "Ophelia" appeared in *Curved Space*, by Susan Terris (La Jolla Poets Press, 1998). Reprinted by permission of the poet.

Lee Upton: "The Ditch" appeared in *Civilian Histories*, by Lee Upton (University of Georgia Press, 2000). Reprinted by permission of the poet.

Lee Upton: "Gertrude to Hamlet" appeared in *Approximate Darling*, by Lee Upton (University of Georgia Press, 1996). Reprinted by permission of the poet.

Ryan G. Van Cleave: "Hamlet at the Paris Aerobleu" is printed by permission of the poet.

Ryan G. Van Cleave: "Ophelia on a Graveled Garden Walk in Purgatory" is printed by permission of the poet.

Jeanne Murray Walker: "How Mother Courage Saves Desdemona" appeared in the *Journal* and in *A Deed to the Light*, by Jeanne Murray Walker (University of Illinois Press, 2004). Reprinted by permission of the poet.

BJ Ward: "Daily Grind" appeared in *Gravedigger's Birthday*, by BJ Ward (North Atlantic Books, 2002). Reprinted by permission of the poet and of North Atlantic Books.

BJ Ward: "Shakespeare as a Waiter" appeared in *Landing in New Jersey with Soft Hands*, by BJ Ward (North Atlantic Books, 1994). Reprinted by permission of the poet and of North Atlantic Books.

William John Watkins: "The Mall" appeared in *SPSM&H*. Reprinted by permission of the poet.

Charles Harper Webb: "At *The Tempest* with a Pregnant Wife" appeared in *River Styx*. Reprinted by permission of the poet.

Jackson Wheeler: "Falstaff's Dream" is printed by permission of the poet.

Gail White: "Queen Gertrude's Soliloquy" appeared in *Mississippi Review*. Reprinted by permission of the poet.

Daniel Williams: "Feste and the Fence Post" is printed by permission of the poet.

Cecilia Woloch: "*Ottava Rima*: Lear" appeared in *Dogwood* and in *Late*, by Cecilia Woloch (BOA Editions, 2003). Reprinted by permission of the poet and of BOA Editions.

David Wright: "Lines on Retirement, after Reading *Lear*" appeared in *Teaching English in the Two-Year College*. Reprinted by permission of the poet.

Tracy S. Youngblom: "Ophelia Speaks" is printed by permission of the poet.

Index